DREAM WALKER

A Journey of Achievement and Inspiration

DR. BERNARD A. HARRIS JR.

with Mickey Herskowitz

GREENLEAF
BOOK GROUP PRESS

Published by Greenleaf Book Group Press
Austin, Texas
www.gbgpress.com

Distributed by Greenleaf Book Group LLC

For ordering information or special discounts for bulk purchases, please contact Greenleaf Book Group LLC at PO Box 91869, Austin, TX 78709, 512.891.6100.

Design and composition by Greenleaf Book Group LLC and Alex Head
Cover design by Greenleaf Book Group LLC

Publisher's Cataloging-In-Publication Data
(Prepared by The Donohue Group, Inc.)
Harris, Bernard A.
    Dream walker : a memoir : a journey of achievement and inspiration / Bernard Harris Jr. with Mickey Herskowitz -- 1st ed.
    p. ; cm.
    ISBN: 978-1-60832-076-9
    1. Harris, Bernard A. 2. African American astronauts--United States--Biography. 3. Physicians--United States--Biography. 4. Self-actualization (Psychology) 5. Conduct of life. I. Herskowitz, Mickey. II. Title.
TL789.85.H37 A3 2010
629.45/0092
2010930029

Part of the Tree Neutral® program, which offsets the number of trees consumed in the production and printing of this book by taking proactive steps, such as planting trees in direct proportion to the number of trees used: www.treeneutral.com

TreeNeutral®

Printed in the United States of America on acid-free paper

10 11 12 13 14 15   10 9 8 7 6 5 4 3 2 1

First Edition

I would like to dedicate this book to my mother (Gussie) and my daughter (Brooke Alexandria), to all the astronauts who came before me, and to the youth of America, who are our future.

Contents

Foreword

Rex Tillerson

Chairman and CEO, Exxon Mobil Corporation

By any measure, Bernard Harris is an authentic American hero. He has inspired his fellow citizens as an astronaut, a physician, an entrepreneur, and as a teacher and mentor for the generations to come.

Dream Walker provides every reader with an invaluable insight into the life of this great American.

Of course, Dr. Harris is best known for his courage in exploring the final frontier. On February 9, 1995, Dr. Harris became the first African-American to walk in space. High above the earth, hurtling at 18,000 miles per hour, he bravely stepped outside the Space Shuttle *Discovery* and into history.

It took years of study, training, and perseverance to achieve his dream. But as we learn from *Dream Walker*, Dr. Harris's walk in space is just one moment in an extraordinary story that has touched lives around the nation.

Long before Bernard Harris floated high above the Earth, he was already striving to make a difference in the lives of others. He began his career as a physician, healing others. After graduating from Texas Tech University School of Medicine,

Harris soon began groundbreaking research in musculoskeletal physiology and then sought training as a flight surgeon and crew medical officer.

After leaving NASA service, Dr. Harris continued to achieve—this time as an entrepreneur and businessman. He became a pioneer and investor in life-saving telemedicine, and he continues to apply the lessons of space travel to improve health care and our knowledge of the human body.

As we learn from *Dream Walker*, Dr. Harris has always been driven by a desire to reach for the stars. From his birth on the plains of Temple, Texas, to his childhood in the Navajo Nation in Arizona and New Mexico, from the University of Houston to the Mayo Clinic and the NASA Space Center, he has never forgotten the importance of education and opportunity in achieving one's dreams.

Dr. Harris now inspires others with his work as a philanthropist. He has funded projects to help America's next generation succeed, and he is providing special outreach to young people from America's urban centers and underserved communities. He speaks eloquently on the importance of math and science to the future of every American. He regularly reminds citizens across the nation that technological innovation is the key to opportunity, to America's continuing competitiveness, and to meeting the world's great challenges in the twenty-first century.

As part of his vision of opportunity for all, Dr. Harris has inspired, funded, and run summer science camps for bright and ambitious middle-school students—especially those from disadvantaged backgrounds. At his science camps, young people receive full scholarships to spend two weeks on a college campus experimenting with, learning, and exploring math and science. Most important, they begin to see the value of education and their own potential to excel.

Over the last three years, Dr. Harris has visited thirty cities from Anchorage to Mobile with his unique Dream Tour, during which he has inspired thousands of young people to pursue their dreams through science, technology, engineering, and mathematics. Just before Christmas in 2009, he gathered ten thousand students in Houston's basketball arena—not for a sporting event, but to cheer math and science achievement.

While traveling on his Dream Tour, Dr. Harris has met with leaders from local governments, schools, and businesses to discuss the importance of education in science, technology, engineering, and mathematics, not only to their own communities but also to our entire nation.

I am proud of ExxonMobil's work with this American hero. We have partnered with Dr. Harris and The Harris Foundation to create the ExxonMobil Bernard Harris Summer Science Camps. And we are proud to sponsor The Dream Tour, which continues to emphasize hope and opportunity through better education.

As readers of *Dream Walker* will learn, the courage and continuing sacrifice of Dr. Harris have strengthened our nation. We salute this American hero, not only for his own accomplishments but also for his commitment to inspiring the next generation of Americans to pursue their opportunities and dreams to become heroes themselves.

Chapter 1

A COLD NIGHT IN HEAVEN

Did you ever see a dream walking?
Well, I did!
Did you ever hear a dream talking?
Well, I did!
—Mack Gordon and Harry Revel

I cannot say for sure if I've ever heard "Did You Ever See a Dream Walking," written for the 1933 film *Sitting Pretty*, or even the remake by Fats Domino in the sixties. But the lyrics certainly reflect my life, especially the line that goes, "Well, I did!"

I lived a dream, walking, floating, and maneuvering in space 250 miles above Earth. We had an international crew that included Vladimir Titov, the Russian cosmonaut whose career at that point included the record for longest endurance flight. The date was February 9, 1995, and we made history three ways: Eileen Collins became the first woman to pilot the space shuttle, and Michael (Mike) Foale became the first Englishman and I the first African-American to walk in space as we ventured outside the man-made environment and friendly confines of the space shuttle *Discovery*. The joy and beauty of that silent night were interrupted only by the fact that Mike and I nearly froze—literally.

The mission included a rendezvous and close flyby of the Russian space station, *Mir*, as well as operation of SpaceHab-3, a commercially developed laboratory module that was making its third flight on the shuttle, carrying more than forty experiments. We would also deploy and retrieve the Spartan-204 satellite, a kind of free-flying platform designed to gather scientific data through ultraviolet light.

The best part of all was that Mike Foale and I were scheduled to take our five-hour stroll in space. How cool was that? It turned out to be much cooler than we expected or wanted.

Our commander, Jim Wetherbee, brilliantly overcame problems with leaky thrusters and managed to fly the shuttle manually to within thirty-seven feet of Mir. We could talk with the cosmonauts aboard and actually wave to them through the hatch windows.

After nearly seven days aboard *Discovery*, orbiting Earth at eighteen thousand miles per hour, and thus circling the globe every ninety minutes, the time had come for our final preparations in the claustrophobic confines of the airlock. We had spent hours focusing on the tasks at hand, eager to do what few astronauts get to do—walk in space.

Mike and I had floated into the airlock wearing only the lower torso units of our space suits pulled over our Liquid Cooling and Ventilation Garments (LCVGs), a kind of spaceman's "union suit." Clear plastic tubing filled with water is integrated into the fabric of the LCVG to control body temperature amid the harshness of space. While in the airlock, we were still connected to the umbilicals that supplied water and air.

Once we were ready, we connected our lower suits to the hard upper torso units and locked the two halves together using the waist seals. We powered up our suits, went through our checklists, and then put on the goofy-looking brown "Snoopy caps" with the built-in mics and earphones that would allow us to communicate with each other, the *Discovery* crew, and Mission Control in Houston.

Snoopy caps have been in use since the *Apollo* days, and I liked the fact that astronauts still wore them. To me, they served as a token of respect for, or at least a palpable connection to, the first moon landing I had watched, wide-eyed, in front of our small black-and-white TV as a thirteen-year-old kid. Now it would be my turn to take a modest leap, if not a "giant" one, of my own.

In the Neutral Buoyancy Lab in Houston, we had rehearsed for months every move we would make aboard *Discovery*. We locked on our gloves and helmets, pressurized the suits up to 4.3 pounds per square inch, and checked them over and over to make sure there were no pressure leaks. The pure oxygen to prevent decompression sickness, commonly known as "the bends," flowed steadily as we waited patiently during our four-hour prebreathing. We smiled as the regulators and fans kicked in to keep us comfortable. We were ready.

With everything a "go," we opened the hatch to the outside. For a brief moment, my mind tried to trick me. I knew we were safe aboard the spacecraft, but suddenly, stepping outside, I felt uneasy. When I had watched people step out of a flying aircraft before, they had been torn away by the wind and dropped like a stone by the force of gravity until the parachute opened. I imagined plummeting through space, all the way to Earth.

As a physician, I am inclined to advise people to trust their bodies. The body never lies. It lets you know when you are in pain, when you are tired, and what nutrients you need. But the mind is a trickster. It is filled with delusion, and it's a sucker for visual tricks.

My reasoning instincts quickly regained control, and my fear melted away. We would be fine; the tether cable was hooked, and there was no gravity. I had been looking forward to this moment for most of my life. The present was all that mattered, and it was time to get on with it.

As I exited the hatch, I understood that I was getting an opportunity that very few people ever have—to see with my own eyes an unobstructed view of Earth from space, to view the beauty and majesty of God's creation in an awe-inspiring panorama. In that moment, nothing seemed impossible. There was a sense of freedom and of something that reminded me of the childhood years I spent on a Navajo reservation: a oneness with the universe.

When we first stepped out for our Extravehicular Activity (EVA in NASA-speak), Janice Voss (the Mission Specialist 3 on board) positioned the robot arm in a way that allowed us to put a special foot restraint on it. Mike slipped into the foot restraint, and I was tethered to him. Next she lifted up the arm and dangled it above the open payload bay, and then we turned on the sensors in our space suits so that we could begin to measure the temperature inside them. Oddly enough, this never had been done before.

Americans had been traveling in space for more than thirty years, yet until our mission, they had never measured the temperature inside their space suits. Many of the space walkers had reported that during the night pass, the period of time when the Earth blocks the light and heat of the sun, it turned so cold that they were unable to move their hands.

Lack of mobility makes it nearly impossible for astronauts to do our jobs. However, since all astronauts seem to truly believe they are invincible, almost superheroes, they just toughed their way through it. Even so, we had all been saying for years that we needed heaters in our gloves, heaters for our extremities, and so forth. But the engineers wanted such data to support these claims, and nobody had ever given it to them.

Mike and I were to be guinea pigs. We were to hang out in space for an hour and a half, the time it took the shuttle to orbit the world, through night and day. We had a special device to measure the ambient temperature, and we had temperature sensors inside our suits at different points. No problem.

Within ten minutes of entering the night pass, the ambient temperature plummeted from 200 degrees Fahrenheit to minus 165. It fell to 20 degrees Fahrenheit inside our suits. Try to imagine taking a stroll outside naked on a 20-degree winter night.

Of course, we were all communicating with one another. NASA has communication protocols. Astronauts talk through a designated person on their spacecraft, and at any time Mission

Control can hear the communication. So Story Musgrave at Mission Control in Houston could listen in to the communication Mike and I had with Eileen Collins, our EVA controller. We had agreed in advance that when the temperature started to fall, they would ask us, "What is your number?" And then we would rate the temperature on a scale of one to five, with five being the worst.

We decided to use this code because we didn't want to be recorded saying something like, "I'm freezing my astronaut butt off!" while millions of people were watching the mission live on television. That would have been the sound bite of the week.

After twenty minutes of the night pass, Eileen said, "Okay, guys, what's your number?" Though we knew we were in trouble, both of us responded with a three. But within five minutes, we both said, "Five!" Somewhat incredulous, Eileen asked, "Five?" And again we said, "Five!"

At that point, the alarm was inescapable. She said, "Houston, this is Eileen. The guys are reporting five." And Story, veteran of four missions at that point, simply replied, "Roger." I suspect the seriousness didn't register with him, because he said nothing else. Eileen made a second call and said, "Say again, we're still at a five."

That time Story's voice jumped. "Five?!" After a pause, he said, "Oh!" and then there was total silence as he keyed the radio off while I'm sure the flight director was saying something like, "What the hell are we going to do?"

We were acting as radiators, releasing what little heat we had. Our extremities were turning into ice sculptures; I felt it especially in my feet. Mike decided that he would use the bit of wiggle room in his pressurized suit to pull his hands out of his gloves. I said to him immediately: "You really don't want to do that. Without your hands in them to provide heat, those gloves are going to get so cold that you'll never be able to slip your hands back in." He could have suffered instant frostbite. If we had encountered another emergency, there would have been nothing he could do. We would have been in a no-win situation.

I chose to keep mine in the gloves and try to increase my internal BTUs (British thermal units, a measure of heat) by moving my hands and legs and arms and trying to generate whatever warmth I could. It was painful, but at least I was able to function.

I could not say then, and am not sure even now, how grim or dangerous our situation was. We could always retreat to the spacecraft if we could overcome our pride and actually, physically, make the necessary moves, but that would have meant not completing the mission, which would mean failure.

Finally, we heard a call from Mission Control instructing the commander to flip the spaceship over so that Mike and I would be tethered no longer above it on the deep-space side, which was colder, but between Earth and the ship. In that way, the radiant heat coming up from Earth could warm us a bit from below and reflect back on us from the shuttle above, so that we immediately could feel some relief from the biting, bitter cold, even during the night passes.

A space maneuver such as this is a beautiful sight even

when you think you're freezing to death. *Discovery* has twenty-three reaction-control jets that fire in sequence, and they sound like cannons going off. We heard *boom-boom-boom*, and then the vehicle slowly began to rotate. One moment the ship was below us, partially blocking our view of Earth. The next moment we seemed to be leading the massive vehicle by our slender leash, swinging it in a delicate arc until it was perfectly positioned above us, revealing the complete panorama of Earth in all its glory.

You might think that in the vacuum of space we wouldn't have been able to hear the jets firing, and you would be right. If we had been floating free, we would have seen them fire, but we would not have been aware of the sound. But since we were attached to the ship by the foot restraint and the tether, we were able to "hear" the explosions as they vibrated through the metal structure of the ship. It was an exciting, terrifying, and beautiful multisensory sound and light show that is burned indelibly in my memory. After several minutes, we began to see a glimpse of the sun appear on the horizon, ushering in the day in orbit and bringing immediate warmth. Since we traveled around the world every ninety minutes, we had a day and a night pass every forty-five minutes. The sunrise was incredible in its speed and brilliance.

During the remainder of the EVA, about three more hours, the ship was kept above us. By then we had begun our other work, which kept us moving and generating more of our own heat. Even though the night passes felt as if we were being massaged with razor blades, we were able to stay outside and achieve our objectives—and complete the mission.

The second part of our space walk was to maneuver the Spartan-204 satellite. We had retrieved it from space with the robot arm. In Earth's gravity, it weighed more than three thousand pounds. I would not have been able to move it even in my dreams. But in the zero gravity of outer space, I was able to move the satellite with one hand. I felt like Superman, although as I recall from my reading of the classics, Superman was vulnerable to neither heat nor cold—only Kryptonite.

—

As a thirteen-year-old, I was captivated by the television series *Star Trek*, by Buck Rogers as a multimedia figure, and by any science-fiction book or movie that crossed my path. My dream to venture into outer space began on July 20, 1969, when I watched the black-and-white television set in our living room, transfixed, as Neil Armstrong and Buzz Aldrin stepped onto the surface of the moon.

There was no earthly—or unearthly—reason for me to believe that becoming an astronaut was a realistic goal. I was a black kid from a broken home, whose mother had left Texas and moved her three children to Arizona and then to New Mexico to accept the only teaching job she could obtain, on a reservation in a town called Greasewood, part of the Navajo Nation. The only astronauts we knew about resembled Armstrong and Aldrin: white, Anglo-Saxon, and former fighter pilots.

At that time, I also saw news coverage from Alabama, Mississippi, Arkansas, and across most of Old Dixie, of deputies turning German shepherds loose on black demonstrators, spraying them with water hoses and flailing at them with clubs.

Mine is a familiar story. I grew up facing considerable challenges, and then went on to fulfill dreams that were seemingly impossible to fulfill. But my story has a twist: I was born in 1956, the year after a black seamstress named Rosa Parks refused to give up her bus seat to a white man in Montgomery, Alabama, and the year before the Russians lobbed *Sputnik*, the rocket whose eerie *beep-beep* sound jolted America's pride, into space. For me, these two events connected in 1962, at Rice Stadium in Houston, when President John F. Kennedy committed the United States to putting a man on the moon within a decade.

Over the decades, astronauts have been at times poetic and at times breezy about their experiences. With the Original Seven, much was written about their view of Earth, without borders or boundaries, a blue and white marble against a backdrop of dark blankness. They could squint and raise a thumb and blot out the entire planet.

Ever since astronauts landed on the moon, and America began sending unmanned probes beyond our universe, humans have talked and written majestically of our journey to other worlds. But from my own perspective, I had lived in more than one world without ever leaving America's rugged southwestern landscape.

In the Navajo community we moved into, there were a few white families, but many of the young Navajo children had never seen blacks. When we first arrived, there was a lot of curiosity about my sister and brother and me. The children enjoyed touching and rubbing our hair, which was so different from their own.

In time I made many Navajo friends. Moving from what had been a poor neighborhood in Houston to the Navajo Nation turned out to be a change of luck in those highly impressionable years. Before long my siblings and I were playing ball and riding bikes with all the kids in the neighborhood.

We attended festivals and tribal dances and learned Navajo history, traditions, and philosophy, which I found especially valuable. The Navajo believe that all living things, from humans and other animals to plants and to Earth itself, have their own spirit, and each spirit is connected to and intertwined with all other spirits. For the Navajo, the purpose of life was to strive for a balance, or *Hozho*, between the individual and the universe, to live in harmony with all of nature and the Creator. *Hozho* made wonderfully good sense to me.

—

My first mission was as a crew member aboard the space shuttle *Columbia*, designated as STS-55, and I was part of the international team training in Germany. I teamed and roomed with Jerry Ross, the payload commander making his fourth spaceflight.

When I learned I had been selected for my first mission, the liftoff was scheduled for the summer of 1992. We didn't launch until April 26, 1993.

I am violating no secrecy act when I say there are no flawless missions. Problem solving, in fact, is an essential part of the challenge. But the abort on our first attempt to launch was hardly business as usual; it was only the second time it had happened in shuttle history. More about the flight of *Columbia* later.

By the time we actually went into space, we had trained for eighteen months, with one scary misadventure followed by delay after delay. I went into quarantine three times, each time thinking: *Am I ever going to go on that freaking flight? Am I ever going to get off the ground? Is it really going to happen?*

Every flight is eventful in one respect or another, and my first flight attempt was heightened by the fact that my wife, Sandra, and I were expecting our first child, a daughter we would name Alexandria. The good news was that the delay ensured I would be on Earth for Alexandria's birth. In fact, she was nearly six months old when we finally launched. These six months gave Sandra the extra time she needed to cope with the doomsday instructions every spouse of an astronaut has to endure. I tried to make it easier for her by placing all our essential documents and paperwork in what we jokingly labeled the "death folder," which she could use to sort out my affairs in case of my death.

There was also a small sidebar to the flight that I thought would remain relatively private. Since the days of *Apollo*, each astronaut has been permitted to take a symbol or an item of sentimental or personal meaning into space. I received permission to take a Navajo flag. I wanted to honor the Navajo Nation, the people who had been a significant part of my life in the years when my character was, in visible ways, being shaped.

When we returned from the mission, I went on the customary media tour, pleased with what we had accomplished and feeling high on life. At our first press conference, I took a question from a reporter in the audience who asked me how I felt about the controversy over the Navajo flag.

It was a punch to the stomach, a blindside hit. I must have looked stunned, because the reporter then immediately asked, "Did you know there was a controversy?" I did not.

It turned out that there is a legend about an evil medicine man, Noqoilpi, or He-who-wins-men (at play). "The Gambler," as he was called in English, wreaked havoc on the Navajo Nation. The united efforts of five or six trusted medicine men were needed to surround him, put a curse on him, and get rid of him by sending him into the heavens, into space or the "stillness," as the Navajo people call the silent region where evil is sent during spiritual ceremonies. As he ascended into exile, he cursed his judges: "I will strike you all down with lightning. I will spread war and disease among you. May the cold freeze you! May the fire burn you! May the waters drown you!" he cried, and he vowed to return one day to again bedevil the Navajo Nation.

I was clearly caught off guard. The reporter took me aside, explained what had happened, and showed me a series of articles that had appeared in the *Navajo Times* while I was in space. I was surprised by what I read. Some of the medicine men believed that by taking the flag into space, I had endangered the Nation. The burning question, it turned out, was whether the flag had been blessed before it went into space.

All I had done was contact the president of the Navajo Nation and ask his permission to take the flag with me to honor the spirit and values of Native Americans. He had thought the idea was great, an honor for the Navajo Nation, and he had presented the idea to the tribal council. I was then given a flag, but not a traditional flag. This one was made out of elements of the Earth, with pollen and minerals that came from the soil of the Nation.

We soon found out that the flag had been blessed. The Navajo president had discussed the "curse" and the "blessing" with the elders and the council, and a medicine man had blessed the flag, but no one had mentioned the ceremony to me. So at a time of celebration, I was made aware once again that we can have an impact on others in many ways and be totally unaware of the consequences.

Years later I was invited back to my elementary school in Greasewood, and the *Navajo Times* came out and interviewed me for a story about returning to my childhood home. But there was one paragraph in the story that raised a question: What has happened to the Navajo flag?

The answer is that it remains in my home. I have not returned the flag to the Nation, but I have had conversations with the Smithsonian about putting it on display there. I've held off donating the flag, though, to avoid recycling the former controversy and potentially troubling my Navajo brothers.

Chapter 2

A Woman's Touch

This is a man's world, this is a man's world
But it wouldn't be nothing, nothing
without a woman or a girl.
—lyrics by James Brown

As a boy I was surrounded by strong, nurturing women, two of whom graduated from college in times when this was not an easy or common experience for women, especially women of color. My great-aunt Helen, my mother's aunt, was the first in the family to receive a college degree, in home economics, setting the standard for the rest of the family. She was what the townsfolk called a "pillar of the community." She taught various grade levels for more than forty years, and all of her students loved "Ms. Helen."

My mother, Gussie Emanuel Harris, earned her bachelor's degree in home economics from Prairie View A&M University, and spent the next few years trying to find a school that would hire her. Teaching jobs were hard to come by; there were only vacancies when someone retired or died. While she searched for a teaching position, she did whatever she could to take care of her family. This experience reinforced in us, her children, the value of acquiring as many skills as you could because you never knew what life had in store for you.

Our grandmother Mary always said, "Bernie is going to be a doctor, Gillette will be a nurse, and Dennis will be a dentist." She nailed two out of three. Pulling teeth didn't appeal to my younger brother, though he did go into the health field, majoring in physical education and gerontology. Dennis now has a successful career in parks and recreation, as an executive director.

My sister, Gillette, should have been the first doctor in the family, but women doctors were still frowned on at the time. She went into nursing instead, earned a master's degree, and then went on to have a fulfilling career. Had she been my age, just six years younger, she might have become a doctor. In any case, I learned from her. My sister was always intelligent, a strong young lady who knew early in life what she wanted. My brother and I knew that there wasn't much she didn't know. And even though we would act out, as boys will do, she kept us in line. Gillette was—is—smarter than I am, and I still consider her one of my role models.

In Houston, we lived in the West End, an area near the Heights, not far from downtown. It was once a neighborhood with a Southern feel and tree-shaded streets with small, wood-framed houses. The section where we lived would nowadays be considered economically disadvantaged, because most of the people who lived there were classified as working class. By the time we moved there, a lot of homes in the area had fallen into disrepair because most of the people struggled to pay their bills and had little left over for upkeep on their homes.

The house where my family lived was bulldozed to make way for Interstate 10 in the 1960s. Construction began in 1960 and was completed in 1968, and the freeway became the northern boundary of the West End and the southern boundary of the Heights. It now rumbles through the old neighborhood amid a constant din of speeding trucks, all of which seem bound for anywhere but there. Still, this part of Houston was once a source of pride to the residents, especially since Dan Rather and A. J. Foyt spent their formative years there.

I left the West End when I was six, when my mother collected the three of us, packed as much of our belongings as she could manage into a large, battered suitcase, and put us all on a Greyhound bus to Temple, in Central Texas, where my grandmother lived.

I remember the coolness of the window glass on my cheek as the bus pulled away from the station. I knew we were leaving Houston and my father, and I didn't expect to see either again. I had vague memories of my parents when they were young, laughing and seemingly happy. Bernard A. Harris Sr. wasn't uncaring or cruel. He was just a well-intended man with a dead-end job who drank too much and too often.

After my mother left my father, she was still determined to find a job teaching. Until then, she settled for working as a cook at a diner in Waco, at first driving thirty miles each way from Temple. Later, we moved to Waco, where we stayed with my aunt Jo, who was a distant relative on my mother's side of the family. Sometimes we visited our great-grandmother, Lizzie, on the family farm in Oakwood, about a hundred miles east of Temple. That farm has been in our family for over a hundred years. As children we loved being at Oakwood. There were trees to climb, fields to explore, and creeks to fish. We had big family gatherings and gorged on home-cooked meals. It was a happy time, even Sundays, which were reserved for church and prayer; working, fishing, and playing were not allowed.

One of the lovely things about being a kid is that for the most part you don't know what you don't have. On our visits to Oakwood, nearly everyone looked like us, and we didn't feel deprived. To this day I often return to the farm my family still owns in Oakwood, just to walk the land, breathe the air, and reconnect with my roots. It's even better if my brother and sister can meet me there. We walk the farm together and sit on the front porch of the old homestead, sharing our thoughts and feelings. It has always been and will remain our very special place.

I am truly grateful that I got to know Lizzie. The granddaughter of slaves, Lizzie Emanuel, known to nearly everyone as "Honey," was a remarkable and fascinating woman. I regret now not asking her to tell me stories about what life was like in the true South.

She had married an older man and raised six children on a cotton and cattle farm in Oakwood that covered 250 acres. My great-grandfather was blinded early in life during an accident while clearing land so that it could be farmed. He later died when the children were teenagers. His death left Honey to finish raising the children and also work the farm. She was savvy enough to keep the farm, while many people lost their land to unscrupulous people, stealing it through various schemes.

Honey was a very spiritual person who lived by her convictions. Everyone respected her for this, whether they agreed with her or not. She was such a firm believer in education that she allowed members of the extended family—and even nonmembers—to live in her home so that they could go to high school if they were not allowed to attend the public school in their own town because of the color of their skin.

My earliest recollection is of sitting in Honey's lap in a rocking chair on her front porch, singing Christian hymns and looking out over the yard, where she grew peas. Another early memory is of her giving me my first cup of coffee. She loved her morning coffee, sweet with real cream, but with more cream than coffee. I can still recall how wonderful it tasted.

Once I ran across records of her marriage and learned that our family migrated to Texas from the Carolinas. I believe they did what many African-Americans of her time would do: They picked Emanuel from the Bible as a surname and dropped the slave owner's name. It was only natural to do this, since many blacks were of deep Christian faith.

Honey was not only a pillar of her family but also a pillar of the community, and many of her neighbors thought of her as a healer. When anybody was sick, they would come to her, and she usually knew how to treat them. Once, there was an accident on the road near her house and a man was bleeding out. A neighbor rushed to fetch Honey and led her to the scene. She kneeled down and put her hands over his wounds and said a prayer with a Bible in her hands. The bleeding stopped and the stranger lived; the word was that she had powers. One way or another, she may have helped plant the thought in me that I could be a doctor; that interest must have come from somewhere.

Honey's spunk, spirit, and perseverance enabled her to do seemingly impossible things. Even with a husband and children to care for, she found time to informally educate herself. Always a pioneer, she was one of the first owners of a Ford Model T for miles around.

My mother had that same perseverance. It was challenging for my mother to live with all of us kids at a relative's house, but she wanted to provide the best she could for us as her marriage fell apart. And though it seemed as if a teaching position would never open up, she continued to send her résumé to schools across the country. She was determined not to work in the diner any longer than she had to.

Sometimes I went with her to the diner in Waco. I could never understand why we were not allowed to enter through the front of the restaurant like everyone else. Instead, we had to use the back door. When I asked my mother why, she said that was simply the way it was. I can only imagine how humiliated she must have felt.

Eventually, my mother found a teaching position. My grandmother had seen an advertisement on the bulletin board at the post office, a posting that said teachers were needed on Native American reservations in the West. Mom applied to the Bureau of Indian Affairs, and soon she left for Oklahoma City for orientation at a Native American school. No one at the Bureau cared what race the teachers were. Mom accepted the position—she was our family's first government employee—and within a week, she was boarding a bus for northeastern Arizona. She had rarely been out of Texas and didn't know a soul in Arizona, but she was determined to succeed.

Within six months, Mom had saved enough money to buy a car, and she came back to Temple to pick up the three of us and take us to Arizona. In letters, she had described the mountainous landscape, scenery that was very unlike that of Central Texas. I pictured jagged mountain peaks covered with green pine trees, except in winter when the mountaintops would be thick with snow. But as we traveled west, it was quite unlike how I had imagined. The only green we saw was in West Texas, where the crops were watered by huge sprinkling systems. Arizona and New Mexico looked like Western movie sets, with plateaus and wonderful vistas. The layers of rock were filled with hues of pink, gold, and gray. The further we traveled, the stranger the names of the towns seemed to get: Cubero, Acomita, Albuquerque.

My curiosity was strong and my perceptions mixed when we arrived among the Navajo in Greasewood, near Window Rock, Arizona. Greasewood seemed too small to be a town, and there was very little activity. Distant mountains surrounded the town, and clumps of grass, cactus, and low shrubs dotted the landscape. Television reception was almost nonexistent, and the nearest "big" town was over a hundred miles away.

I remember my first day of elementary school, being introduced to the class. All of the Navajo kids were sort of standoffish because they had never seen an African-American. Silently, they gathered around me on the playground, looking closely at me and at my skin, and touching my hair.

Gillette was in junior high school, but the schools within a commutable distance only went up to the sixth grade. Mom had assumed that there would be classes for students all the way through the senior year and had not thought to ask. She sent Gillette back to Texas to live with Honey.

It took a while for me and Dennis to assimilate. We were unsure at first, but we quickly learned to love being in Greasewood. As our peers learned to accept us, we learned their culture. We grew up believing in werewolves, trusting in medicine men (native healers), and going to rain dances and snake dances. This was the first time that I had explored a unique culture and people. It was eye-opening for me not only to see but also to live in a world so different from my own.

But the most important thing I took from that experience was the connection to the Earth, to the spirit of the universe. The Navajo believe in the sanctity of life and nature. It is an integral part of their being. Through knowing the Earth, you discover its spirit and God. This was an important lesson that I now use in my own life.

The second most important thing I learned was the skill

of living in a multicultural environment, among not only the Native Americans, who were in the majority, but also the white kids, who were mainly the children of government workers, and the Hispanic Americans.

We moved to Tohatchi, in New Mexico, when I was eleven, and the harmony celebrated by the Navajo was beginning to embrace us. We had now been accepted by the native people, and we were accepting of them. This made the transition this time much easier. In addition, we had moved closer to the "big" city of Gallup, New Mexico, so we now had TV reception!

It was in the living room of our home in Tohatchi that I watched on television as Neil Armstrong and Buzz Aldrin stepped onto the surface of the moon in July 1969. I had just turned thirteen years old in June. As I watched these guys step out of the lunar lander and heard Armstrong say the words: "One small step for man, one giant leap for mankind," it was a giant leap not only for mankind but also for this little boy, who looked at that black-and-white television and said, "I want to be an astronaut!" In that moment, I was touched in both my head and my heart. My head saw how exciting it was to be an astronaut. When you returned you were hailed a "hero." And I wanted to be an American hero, too. Like many kids in my day, my heart was also touched by the notion of flying in space—it made me feel good. I felt as though I were meant to do this. That feeling has remained to this day.

More and more, I became secure about the idea of someday joining the space program. I set my goal: to become an astronaut.

With rare exceptions, I kept my dream a secret. I didn't want anyone to discourage me and tell me I couldn't do it.

My mother decided to obtain a master's degree at Texas Southern University in Houston by taking classes during the summer breaks from the reservation school. Each summer, we returned to Houston and lived with Ms. Helen so that Mom could take classes at TSU. We also visited my grandmother in Temple. It was during one of those trips back to Temple that my mother met—and soon fell in love with—a man named Joe Roye Burgess, who would change all our lives. He was a police officer, a strapping man at six feet two and 240 pounds, who left his job in Temple and followed my mother to New Mexico, joining the force in Gallup. He had self-confidence, an air of authority, and a strong belief in discipline, all of which I sorely needed. I was entering my teenage years at the time, and like most boys that age, I had begun to show signs of independence.

Years later, when I had reconciled with my birth father, who had sworn off drinking and become a lay preacher, it pleased me to hear him say, "Thank God for Joe Burgess!" Joe took over where my father had left off. He provided the discipline and strength of a man, which is important when you are raising two boys. We now had a father who would always be there to pick us up when we fell and push us when we doubted our own abilities. Even though neither of our parents told us in words that they loved us, we knew through their actions.

Eventually, the stars aligned and the timing seemed right to leave the desert and the isolation of the Native American reservation and to settle again in a large and bustling city. Gussie and Joe chose San Antonio, and the family made a glad return to Texas. Jobs were more available at that time, Gillette was in college, and they wanted their two boys to attend high school in a big city.

Dennis was the athlete in the family, a fine basketball player. I was tall but skinny, and lacked the size to compete in football. In my case, I suppose it is fair and true to say that, all my life, I didn't want to use my physical strength against people. I wanted to listen to people, to help and heal them. I was more inclined to use my intellect to discover things and to create opportunities to help myself and others. I discovered very early my love for science and science fiction. I particularly loved to work on science projects, such as building rockets and dissecting things. (I will leave it at that.)

When I was twelve, I discovered I had a talent for music and could play any instrument I picked up. During junior high school in Tohatchi, I learned to play about six different instruments. In part, I had to do this because the school was so small; we all had to learn how to play different instruments in order to give concerts. Now in San Antonio, I focused only on the saxophone. The high school yearbook shows me proudly holding my tenor sax. I even thought for a short while about music as a career. So I formed a band with some friends. We called ourselves the Purple Haze, after the popular song by Jimi Hendrix. We were lucky that our parents were clueless that "purple haze" referred to getting high. Not too long after the band formed, we began playing nightclubs and special events around the San Antonio area. I had an extremely large Afro, and we all wore bell-bottoms and polyester shirts. We were the quintessential seventies soul band. We even won the Battle of the Bands, a local competition that attracted the city's best bands. The band was fun, and the gigs paid well. It was refreshing to earn our own pocket money.

Throughout this time, I still followed the space program, the way fans follow the box scores of their favorite baseball teams. The astronauts of *Apollo 13* survived their dangerous mission, with Jim Lovell's terse description, "Houston, we've had a problem here," entering the library of famous phrases. NASA launched Skylab, the first American space station, to measure man's ability to live and work in space for long periods of time. Dr. Joe Kerwin, a physician, was one of the first three astronauts to work aboard Skylab. He became another of my role models when he rode an *Apollo* spacecraft up to Skylab with Charles Conrad Jr. and Paul Weitz and docked in May 1973. For twenty-eight days, Dr. Kerwin made medical observations about humans living in a microgravity environment, paving the way for everyone else who has since flown into space.

I knew I needed to major in a science to become an astronaut. I chose medicine because I had always wanted to help others, and also because an African-American physician in San Antonio, Dr. Frank Bryant, inspired me to look into the health professions. A fairly notable guy in the medical field, Dr. Bryant showed me what a day in his professional life was like, and he introduced me to medical students. I was immediately inspired. I thought, *Wow! I can put my two dreams together.* I knew that one of the goals of the space program was to enable people to live in space. And when this happened, these people would need someone to take care of them. I decided then and there to become an astronaut. Of course, I had to become a physician first. Dr. Bryant opened that door to me.

—

On any list of simple pleasures, the ability to surprise your friends and yourself ranks high. One day I used my computer to look up my birthplace, Temple, Texas, to determine if I might find anything interesting for background material for this book.

I have to confess that even a rocket scientist—and some of us actually are—still can be awestruck at the instant access we have to information on the Internet. There was nothing to it. In a blink, I had found a locator map of Central Texas with the town's latitude and longitude, plus detailed descriptions of industry, demographics, transportation systems, and practically everything else anyone could possibly want to know about Temple.

On the town's unofficial home page, under the heading "Notables," I learned that Temple is the hometown of football legend Mean Joe Greene, actor Rip Torn, comedian Bill Engvall, author Bryan Burrough, and (pretend you don't know what's coming) astronaut Dr. Bernard Harris.

I still have to pinch myself on occasion when such things

happen. Growing up, I never thought of myself as becoming "notable," much less as someone who would be listed alongside famous athletes, authors, or movie stars. Those early times in Texas were more notable for challenges than for aspirations to fame or celebrity.

Gussie, Bernard's mother, shortly after her marriage to Bernard Sr.

Gillette (six), Bernard (six months), and Gussie in
their first home in Houston, TX

Bernard Sr. and Jr. in Houston, TX

Gillette (eight), Dennis (one), and Bernard (two) on Bass Street in Houston, TX, on the West End

Dennis, Gillette, and Bernard outside their apartment in Greasewood, AZ

Dennis and Bernard with classmates in Greasewood, AZ

Bernard, age nine, in Greasewood, AZ

Native American dance at a parade in Gallup, NM

Bernard, age thirteen, at Tohatchi Middle School in Tohatchi, NM

Mary C. Culpepper, Bernard's grandmother, in Temple, TX

Joe Roye Burgess, Bernard's stepfather, as a police officer in Temple, TX, 1965

The Purple Haze band in San Antonio, TX

Bernard at graduation from Sam Houston High School in San Antonio, TX

Chapter 3

EXPANDING MIND

Whether you think that you can or that
you can't, you are usually right.
—Henry Ford

Who would guess that some of the most helpful advice I have ever received came from a twelve-year-old? During one of our childhood summer trips to Houston, I befriended Cleverick Johnson, who lived across the street from my great-aunt Helen in a part of Houston called Sunnyside.

Sunnyside sat in the heart of Houston's black community. My aunt's home was in a new, middle-class neighborhood. Many of our neighbors were professionals: teachers, preachers, and lawyers. There were a good many role models to draw from, but the person who had the most lasting influence on me was Cleverick.

We were the same age, but he was a city kid, and I had been living in a time warp among the Navajo. One day he and I were sitting on the curb, contemplating what we would do next, when we began to talk about the future.

"What are you going to do when you grow up?" I asked. He

said that he wanted to be a dentist. I volunteered nothing of my dream of becoming an astronaut. I said only that I enjoyed science and that I wanted to make a lot of money.

My response prompted him to ask, "What do you think is a lot of money?"

I thought about my answer for a while, and then I said, "If I had ten thousand dollars, I'd be rich."

"Ten thousand dollars?" he repeated, his voice skeptical. "That's not a lot of money."

"Okay," I said, making a quick adjustment. "Then one hundred thousand dollars. That would do it for me."

He said, "Is that all? You're not thinking big enough."

I asked, "Well, what do *you* think is a lot of money?"

He replied, "A million dollars. No, *ten* million dollars."

As I sat there thinking about the magnitude of his answer, for the first time in my life I realized that I was thinking too small. My whole concept of big money was dwarfed by his. Why? Because I had no frame of reference. From then on, not only was my perception of wealth broadened; my understanding of the world expanded too. Cleverick's simple question opened my mind to think on a different scale. It was the first time—but not the last—that someone suggested to me that the sky was the limit.

When we made our permanent move back to Texas, I was confronted with changes I had had little reason to grapple with in the past. San Antonio was not what most people would have considered a sophisticated city, but life there was so much faster than on the reservation. Sam Houston was an inner-city high school with drugs and violence, the problems so many schools still have today. My mother and Joe would not allow us to be part of that scene. They let us know what was expected of us, and they made it clear that they never wanted to get a call from school or anywhere else about one of us kids getting into trouble. Joe had taught us to respect others and the law, and to never take anything that wasn't ours.

I was fortunate to have my music. Playing in a band with my friends helped me connect with other people, helped my self-confidence, and helped me hear the soft notes some might miss. I loved the music of Charlie Bird and Dizzy Gillespie, but also Kool and the Gang, Earth, Wind & Fire, and James Brown. I especially loved jazz, which is descended from the blues, the soul music of Africa.

Just below the surface lurked my long-term goals. I was an observer of the two continuing stories of that time: the space race with Russia, and the *race* between two Americas. In Arizona and New Mexico, we were not really directly exposed to the civil rights movement. But I have no doubt that the careers I craved, the hand I was dealt, resulted from the sacrifices of those who knocked down the barriers on campuses and offices and diners across the land, and spilled their blood in the deep South.

The great heavyweight champion Joe Louis, the black man cheered by white America when he knocked out Germany's Max Schmeling, was once scolded by civil rights leaders for not being more involved in the cause. Joe replied, quietly: "Some march. Some shout. Some give lots of money. I do it my way, by behaving. All ways help." His message was huge: At a tipping point in history, you could participate by setting an example, by succeeding.

My siblings and I were brought up to believe that education was the best and quickest way out of the slums and the street-corner classrooms that often lured society's underdogs. There was no choice in our family but to go to college. My sister, brother, and I are the third generation of my family to graduate from college.

I was fortunate to know what my major would be long before I enrolled at the university. When I arrived at the University of Houston in 1974, I declared my major as biology/premed. Selecting a major was the easy part. Getting through school with all the distractions was the daunting challenge.

For better or worse, I was involved very early with fraternity life. During the first week on campus, I met the men of Kappa Alpha Psi. They not only threw the best parties but also were focused on achievement. There were nine African-American college-based fraternities. All had similar goals: to support young students who would excel in academics, graduate, and become productive citizens. But the Kappas were special: Their emphasis was on graduation from college as well as on "achievement in every field of human endeavor." This was their motto. They were promoting success in young men very much like me.

One of those who stood out during my freshman year was Gerald McElvy, a junior who was a resident dorm adviser, which meant he was a student leader whose role was to keep the younger guys out of trouble. Gerald went on to become an accounting executive with ExxonMobil and the president of the ExxonMobil Foundation, moving from Texas to New Jersey to Australia in a career that has spanned more than thirty years. We forged a bond that endured, and in time he would be a supporter of the math and science camps I founded years after I left NASA.

—

The University of Houston was one of the first major colleges in Texas to racially integrate its sports teams. The Cougars gained national prominence in football, under Coach Bill Yeoman, and went head-to-head against UCLA in basketball, under Guy Lewis. But outsiders were slow to recognize the progress that was being made in academics.

When you declared premed as a major, you inevitably had to meet Dr. Catherine Cominsky, the premed adviser. She was an intimidating woman who tolerated no nonsense when it came to qualifying for medical school. As some put it, she took no prisoners. If you were not yet serious about the program, you were out. You had to be committed. I was, but as with most new college students, there were other interests that tugged at me, such as girls and good times.

There are two kinds of students: those who, years later, look back and say, "I wish I had studied more and partied less," and those who say, "I wish I had studied less and partied more." I walked a very fine line. I wish I could say I resisted and did not fall victim to the social temptations of college life. But I would be lying. Still, I am here to say that you can survive despite yourself.

After three years at the University of Houston, the time came to apply to medical school. I started out with a list of fifteen schools, but when I found out how much it cost to apply to each school, the list was whittled down to six. I was lucky to be selected for interviews with three Texas medical schools. In the end, I was Texas Tech's choice, and it was mine. Lubbock was in the heart of West Texas, home to cotton fields, oil rigs, and cowboys; it seemed like the last place an African-American student would want to go.

In 1978, the first groups of astronaut candidates for the Space Shuttle program were selected. It was the same year I received my bachelor's degree and was accepted into medical school. The timing, the connection, were not lost on me, and Lubbock was where I would fulfill my dream of becoming a doctor; it was my launching pad into medicine.

—

Tech definitely was one of the places that molded me. During orientation, I met a fellow student, Michael (Mike) Robertson, who became my lab partner and my friend for life. For the next four years, this other aspiring doctor and I worked and studied together and boosted each other's morale as needed.

I didn't talk directly with Mike about being an astronaut, but once in a while I dropped my guard or dropped a hint; maybe

I couldn't always contain myself, or maybe I wanted to test his reaction. He never questioned my knowledge about space, but at times I suspected that he thought I was a nutcase. Yet, friend that he was, he would always support me, no matter how crazy my ideas were.

Mike didn't find out about my real aspirations until years later, in 1988 or 1989, in an unusual situation in his office. Here's how he describes that afternoon:

> My receptionist came back into my private office, and her eyes were big as silver dollars. She said, "Dr. Robertson, there is someone here from the FBI, and he wants to talk to you. What have you done?"
>
> As it turned out, it was a federal agent doing a background check on Bernard. He had given them my name. That was really the first inkling I had that he was getting ready to take the next step.

Let there be no doubt: Medical school tested everyone's resolve, including mine. I certainly wondered what I had gotten myself into while cramming late at night for exams. Plus there were the countless hours hovering over a cadaver, trying to decide what some particular structure of the body was. Everyone knew who the freshmen medical school students were by the smell of formaldehyde that lingered in our clothes and skin from the gross anatomy lab. Like everyone else, I grew used to it, even to the point that I didn't notice the smell and could actually eat a tuna fish sandwich during a dissection.

In 1981, as I was launching my career as a physician, I watched the news reports as space shuttle *Columbia* completed its orbits and landed smoothly back on Earth. I wasn't quite ready to be an astronaut, but I knew that I needed to figure out a way to narrow the distance if I was going to join this select group.

During my last year at Texas Tech Medical School, I chose to do all my elective courses at other medical institutions. I spent time in Hawaii with Dr. Robert Overlock, a former Navy SEAL who, in 2000, became medical director of the University of Hawaii's Hyperbaric Treatment Center, and is a family practitioner. The time I spent with him was invaluable. He taught me how to deep-sea dive. Can you imagine being taught how to scuba dive by a former Navy SEAL? The experience was incredible.

I also did preceptorships at Baylor College of Medicine, Harvard, and the Mayo Clinic. All that I learned and absorbed helped me decide which residency I would apply for.

There are not many shortcuts for the doctor-in-waiting; four years of undergraduate work are followed by four more of medical school, then an internship and a residency in a chosen specialty. I chose to do my residency in internal medicine at the Mayo Clinic in Rochester, Minnesota. I wanted to learn all I could about the systems of the human body so that when I went into space I would recognize the changes that a microgravity environment causes.

I knew that completing this residency would help establish my abilities and my perseverance. The Mayo Clinic is a splendid place to hone one's skills. I caught a big break when my resident adviser turned out to be Dr. Ed Rosenow. Dr. Rosenow was a world-renowned pulmonary medicine physician. He was responsible for guiding the careers of many residents at the Mayo clinic. I feel extremely blessed to have had him as my mentor.

While I studied at the Mayo Clinic, the space shuttle program was making history. Guion (Guy) Bluford, Fred Gregory, and Ron McNair joined a shuttle crew in 1978 as the first African-Americans. Three Russian cosmonauts stayed in space for an astounding 237 days, and many other countries were launching communication satellites, making the program truly international.

At Mayo, my first clinical rotation was rheumatology. As a newly minted doctor, the last thing you want to happen is to end up on a really hard rotation such as the cardiac intensive care unit (CICU), where the demands are extremely challenging because most of the patients are in critical condition. Though rheumatology has its moments, the pressure is nothing compared to the CICU. So, from a resident's standpoint, I won the rotation lottery. But, unknown to me, the victory was ever more significant because of my consultant, which is how professors are labeled at Mayo. I drew the best of the best, Dr. Joseph Combs, a physician who had worked with NASA during the most critical times in space history.

After visiting the patients each morning, the residents and

the consultants would sit down over coffee to discuss the cases. This was when we collected the medical pearls from the experienced doctors. It was when they passed on their wisdom to the inexperienced doctors like me. During one of these times, the topic abruptly changed from rheumatology to space exploration. I found out then that Dr. Combs had previously worked for NASA and was one of the doctors responsible for taking care of the astronauts after they returned from the early missions.

The minute I heard of Dr. Combs's experience, I began to reaffirm my desire for a career in space. Up until that point, my dreams had resulted in my decision to pursue medicine as a vocation, so I'd had to be focused exclusively on becoming a physician rather than an astronaut. That first discussion with Dr. Combs led to many others, including the details of his involvement with the early *Gemini* and *Mercury* programs, when men blasted into space, testing the boundaries of human endurance.

To be in the presence of someone who was actually a part of history was awesome—and inspiring. That is exactly what Dr. Combs did for me; he inspired me to accelerate the pursuit of my dream. He gave legs to my ambition and, through his counsel, set me on the road to NASA.

Once he understood my commitment to the dream, he introduced me to the head of the Mayo Clinic Aerospace Medicine program. I recall sitting in the director's office, discussing my future from my perspective.

"After I complete my residency," I confided, "I would like to apply to the astronaut corps and later fly on the space shuttle."

I talked to him with a confidence that was hardly merited, but one I felt nevertheless.

After becoming convinced that I was serious, he looked at me and said, "Wait a minute." Then he turned around at his desk, looked at his Rolodex, and picked up the phone, immediately dialing NASA headquarters. "I have a young man in my office who is interested in becoming an astronaut. What should he do?"

He relayed to me what was said. In order to be noticed, given the sheer number of applicants who apply, you need to make yourself stand out. The best way to do this is by first becoming an expert in an area that NASA needs for future space missions.

I left his office wondering how I was going to do this. After all, I didn't know NASA's needs. So I researched the problem and came to the conclusion that out of all the knowledge needed and currently lacking, the study of bone metabolism—in particular, the development of osteoporosis—was going to be my field of expertise. I soon found mentors at Mayo to assist me in developing a research career: Dr. Lawrence Riggs, a nationally recognized authority in osteoporosis; Dr. Heinz W. Wahner, a pioneer in techniques for the measurement of bone mineral and body composition by photon or X-ray absorptiometry, particularly the dual photon bone densitometer; and Dr. Pasquale J. Palumbo, who held the chair in endocrinology.

After completing my residency at the Mayo Clinic, I returned to San Antonio to begin practicing medicine. After all the years of study and sacrifice, it was good to settle down in a town that I knew well. I was back where I had finished my schoolboy days, where I had spent so many happy nights as a member of the Purple Haze.

One of the little remarked rewards of medicine is the freshness of your cases. Young or old, rich or poor, known or unknown—you can almost never predict who will walk through the door. One afternoon a gentleman came in complaining of an earache. I examined him and found an infection. The patient looked familiar to me, but I couldn't place him. After he left, I looked at his name again in the appointment book and realized that he had been my civics teacher in high school, Mr. Steven Johnson. It was certainly ironic that I had returned home as a "real doctor," practicing real medicine . . . on my civics teacher.

I was in a good place, a familiar place, doing one of the things I loved—and waiting for the phone to ring.

Chapter 4

A Time to Choose

Talent does what it can; genius does what it must.
—Edward George Bulwer-Lytton

From the time I was thirteen, virtually every move I made had been weighed against one consuming question: Would this change draw me closer to flying in space? Becoming an astronaut was more than a dream or a desire; it was my secret obsession. I could relate to Captain Ahab and his great white whale.

One day in 1985 the phone rang in my office in San Antonio, and I suddenly found myself with a dilemma. The National Research Council had called to offer me a NASA fellowship. I had never allowed myself to entertain any doubts, any conflict. I believed I was destined to overcome the odds of a lifetime and qualify for the space program. With the fellowship offer, a crucial step along that path was mine for the taking—and yet I hesitated. I enjoyed being a doctor, having a schedule, being my own boss. There was nothing phony about helping the ill get well, relieving someone of pain, making someone's life easier. And I was comfortable in San Antonio, with its River Walk and diverse population and that historic monument, the Alamo—a constant reminder that moral victories do exist.

I could not have imagined that the choice would be so difficult, until I was faced with actually making it. Should I take a number, get in line, and then try to become an astronaut? Or should I stay in San Antonio and build my medical practice, enjoying the security and respect the profession offered?

I needed someone to discuss this life-changing decision with. Gillette and Dennis agreed to meet me in Oakwood during the Christmas holidays. It was time to walk the land our grandparents had settled. They listened as I recited the pros and cons of each option. Then my sister said, "Do what you think is best; do what your heart tells you." The vexing question was, If I didn't go, would I look back later in life and have regrets?

I accepted the fellowship, but a funding hitch delayed my departure. Finally, nearly six months after that walk in Oakwood, I was in my car driving to the NASA Ames Research Center at Moffett Field, in California's Silicon Valley. There I found another mentor and sponsor for my research, Dr. Sara Arnaud, a nationally recognized expert in calcium metabolism.

My research would be in musculoskeletal physiology and osteoporosis. Living in space causes major changes in the human body and loss of bone density. If people were to live on space stations for long periods of time, better ways to maintain health through exercise and nutrition had to be found.

I met Dr. Arnaud and became a key member of her research team. The time, patience, and discipline that she provided enabled me to acquire the right skills as a researcher and would bring me closer to my dream of working at NASA.

My first task in her laboratory was to participate in a team project to conduct a necropsy on twenty-five rhesus monkeys from a recently completed research study. This may have been the worst job I ever had. The ickiness was off the charts. But doctors cannot be squeamish (and neither can astronauts). As I had in medical school, I put my feelings aside and did my job, one that other scientists and doctors had done on countless occasions in the past. I knew that the research was my ticket into a new life in the space program.

This experience was followed by endless hours in the lab, analyzing tissue and blood samples for factors, elements, and DNA. Many of these I was learning about for the first time. Not since my first day in medical school had I felt so unprepared. Dr. Arnaud was a stickler on laboratory safety, and her team adhered to her rules—or else. Many of the chemicals used in the process could cause cancer in the long term and explosions in the short term if handled improperly.

One day we heard the news of an accident in another lab, in which a young scientist was killed while purging a respiratory system with nitrogen. Nitrogen is used as an agent to clean pumping systems. In most cases, it is safe as long as there is proper ventilation. In his case, he was flushing a space helmet with the nitrogen and forgot to also flush with air before putting it on. Within seconds of placing the helmet on his head, he passed out, suffocated, and died. We all learned the lessons of safety that day as the story traveled around the center. This was a serious business that we were in, and there was no room for fooling around.

The rest of my stay at Ames was devoted to studying the field of endocrinology—in particular, bone and calcium metabolism. The highlight of my training was the well-known bed-rest studies. The NASA Ames Research Center was noted for its famous bed-rest unit, the only self-contained human bed-rest facility in the country, where volunteers were placed in bed for periods of time ranging from one month to one year. Bed rest is the closest way to simulate the effect of weightlessness on the human body on Earth. Scientists had discovered that with the body in a prone position, if you tilted the head down to minus six degrees, the body's response would come close to that of spaceflight. This caused the blood in the legs to shift toward the head just as it does in space. The shift causes a cascade of events that eventually produce changes in the body. These changes are now documented and have set the foundation for the study of space medicine. I was right in the middle of this development, a pioneer in a new field of medicine. It was an exciting time.

NASA Ames Research Center had the only self-contained human bed-rest facility in the country. I was excited to be a part of the bed-rest studies and to meet icons of the space program such as Dee O'Hare, the flight nurse who was responsible for all barbaric medical testing depicted in the movie *The Right Stuff*. My job was to assist in the recruitment of volunteers for our study. I thought that trying to convince people to sign up for a study where they lie in bed all day would be challenging. To my surprise it was not. We had people begging to participate. Why? Many wanted to contribute to science and the space program. Of course, the fact that they were paid for twenty-four hours of work each day also helped. For the most part, they were teachers who were off in the summer when the one- to two-month studies were performed, as well as others who simply thought curling up in bed seemed like nice work. We were grateful to each of them, no matter what the reason. During the bed-rest research, we made major strides in understanding human space adaptation.

Something else happened during my time at Ames: I met Sandra Lewis. When I first noticed this beautiful, green-eyed young lady, I asked around, and a colleague told me that she was working as an administrative assistant for one of the other labs while she finished her business degree at San Jose State. I saw her off and on in the cafeteria, and then a few weeks after I had first spotted her at the research center, a mutual friend introduced us in the library. I think a little matchmaking was going on.

I confessed that I had first seen her about two weeks after I arrived at Ames, when I pulled into a space next to a red Ferrari in the parking lot of a 7-Eleven. I'd glanced over and saw one of the most stunning women I had ever seen. I remember saying to myself, *God, I would like one of those.* (I wouldn't have minded having the Ferrari, either.) But she was holding a pretty little girl in her lap, and a guy got out of the car and walked into the store. Sandra confirmed that she had been the lady in the car; the girl was her godchild, and the man driving the car was just a friend.

Sandra also admitted later that she had noticed me in the cafeteria and thought I was "handsome" (her word, not mine). She assumed I had a wife or girlfriend. Then she saw that I was wearing yellow argyle socks and figured that no one was helping me dress, so I must be single.

We talked and arranged our first date. I picked her up at her home, and we had dinner at the Fish Market in Santa Clara. We talked for what seemed like hours.

After that first date, we became an item both around the center and away from it, enjoying all that California has to offer: sun, mountains, beaches, and countryside. It was a wonderful time. We discovered that we had many interests in common: our families were close-knit, we liked music and sports, and we especially enjoyed each other's company. We soon fell in love.

Meanwhile, after spending a year or so conducting clinical research, I decided that it was time to apply to the astronaut corps. So, in the fall of 1986, I put in my application to NASA's Astronaut Office. I met all the qualifications: I had an advanced degree, and my residency in internal medicine, along with my Ames fellowship, served as experience in the field.

By chance, one of my neighbor's aunts was visiting her, and she invited me to a house party in the apartment complex where I was living. Her aunt turned out to be a manager at NASA headquarters, in Washington, DC. I began to talk about my desire to work for NASA once I completed my fellowship and told her that I was particularly interested in becoming an astronaut. She advised me what to do and made a call to the director of the Equal Opportunity Office at the Johnson Space Center, Dr. Joe Atkinson. It turned out that he was on the astronaut selection committee.

In February 1987, I arranged a meeting with Dr. Atkinson. After we talked, he scheduled a number of meetings for me with various people that same day. I must have made a favorable impression, because several weeks later, I was asked to return to Houston for an official interview for the astronaut corps.

The process was grueling. They invited about thirty of us during my session for a one-week, no-holds-barred process that included medical tests from hell. Every day we were asked to show up at different labs across the base, where scientists and physicians poked and prodded us to find out whether we had the right stuff. All I know is that they took a lot of stuff out of us. God knows what they did with it.

In addition, there were psychological evaluations to determine if we were mentally stable, had epilepsy, or became claustrophobic. Throughout that week, we had the opportunity to meet several astronauts and senior managers during planned events. We all knew these events were part of the interview process. They wanted to see the candidates in different scenarios to test our mettle. Of course, there was also the formal interview by the selection committee.

These interviews were always held in a room in the crew quarters where the astronauts are kept during quarantine, which is at the back of the base, protected from the prying eyes of the media. At that point, I had successfully interviewed for medical school, residency, and the research fellowship, but somehow this interview was different. The outcome could result in my ascent into space, the fulfillment of my dream.

As I walked into the room, all eyes were on me. The only person I knew was Dr. Atkinson, who was sitting directly across from me at this huge T-shape table that occupied the middle of the room. The chair for the interviewee was positioned right at the intersection of the two parts of the table. I sat down in the center, facing the thirteen-person committee.

On the committee were the head of the division, the chief of the astronaut office, the center director, senior managers, and experienced astronauts. It was intimidating and a little stressful. I got the feeling that they were trying to see how I would react under pressure. It was a little like being a lobster lowered into boiling water. I survived to celebrate the end of a long week by attending a barbeque at Pete's, a well-known astronaut hangout.

I returned to NASA Ames Research Center feeling good about how I had done during the interviews. I also had passed the medical examination with flying colors. At that point, I knew I had a good chance of being selected. The timing seemed perfect. I had completed my medical and research training just in time to step into the astronaut corps. I remember thinking that my plan was going to work out.

Before I left Houston, I filled out all the necessary forms, and then I waited for investigations into my background to start. I had no idea that the background check would include face-to-face interviews with my family and friends, who at that point had no idea that I was applying to the astronaut corps—although they should not have been surprised, given my love of all things space.

When an FBI agent contacted my mother, she found out for the first time how serious I was about being an astronaut. She called me long distance and said, "Bernard Anthony Harris Jr., there was a man here with a badge asking me questions about you. What have you done?" When my mother calls me by my full name, I am in trouble, and I know that I had better tell her the whole truth.

So I told her, in detail, about my dream and desire to travel into space. There was silence on the other end of the phone.

"Are you sure this is what you want to do?" she asked.

I said, "Absolutely!" Noting my resolve that day, she never again doubted my passion for space, even though she was fearful for me. After all, not many months before, we had witnessed what happens when things go wrong: The *Challenger* had exploded seconds after liftoff.

Early that spring I was in the laboratory when I received the call from Johnson Space Center's deputy director, Dr. Carolyn Huntoon. I took a deep breath; the call was, I thought, a good sign.

She began by saying, "Bernard, I wanted to let you know that you were not selected." She followed this statement by describing the statistics around the selection process. I am afraid that the only thing I really heard was that I was not selected.

Gradually, what Dr. Huntoon said at the end of our conversation began to register. "We want to offer you a job here at the center," she said. *What? Where?* "You will be working in the Medical Sciences Division. I know that this is not what you wanted, but it does provide you the opportunity to work for NASA and perhaps apply again."

"Thank you," I said before hanging up the phone. She took that to be a yes.

I did not have a great deal of experience with rejection and how to handle it. At that instant, California seemed a lonely place, far away from my friends and family. I needed someone to talk with, and there was only one person I could count on—Sandra. She remembers how I showed up at her door "looking really dejected." I needed a sympathetic ear. She supported me during that difficult time and cheered me when I was down. For this I will thank her forever.

—

In 1987, my research fellowship drew to a close. The *Challenger* tragedy had not shaken my faith in the space industry. As I contemplated the life that awaited me in Houston and my new position, there were a number of questions in my mind. The topmost of these: What more could I possibly do to qualify to become an astronaut?

I moved back to Texas as a clinical scientist and researcher for the Johnson Space Center. I reported to Dr. Victor Schneider, the leading NASA expert in bone loss and osteoporosis.

Once again I was lucky, or maybe blessed. Dr. Schneider not only taught me about the field of space medicine but also was both a mentor and a friend. During our first meeting, he wrote the word "paranoid" on the blackboard behind his desk, and then drew a circle around it and a line through the center, like a no-smoking sign. He was right; working for the government you had to guard against paranoia unless, as Victor said, someone is really out to get you. With all the competing scientists, divisions, departments, and centers, it could be a dangerous place for a young scientist.

Sandra had encouraged me to take the job, even though she was disappointed to see me leave California. We both knew it was best for her to finish her degree, and there would be time for us to be together again in the future.

When I came back that next summer for her graduation, I proposed. She asked me how the weather was in Houston, and I lied to her. "Nice! Just like California." As luck would have it, the week she visited me, in October, the weather was perfect. It was a rare autumn week in Houston: sunny, with a cool breeze and not a trace of humidity.

We were married on July 22, 1989. Sandra forgave me for not sharing that living in Houston felt like enduring a tropical heat wave most of the year. She had an old turbo Volvo, a classic, boxy model with leaky oil rings. Each time she started the engine, oil leaked into the manifold and smoke billowed out. We decided to drive it back to Houston anyway, and we pulled away from her mom's house in a cloud of black smoke. Even as a newlywed, my bride was not high maintenance, but her car sure was. She kept the Volvo another five years, pouring money into it for repair after repair.

As soon as she moved to Houston, Sandra began job hunting. We lived close to the Texas Medical Center, which was not too far of a commute from the NASA offices in Clear Lake, on the south side of Houston. She went out looking for a job every day, and one day she had to drive my convertible, a tiny Fiat Spider that I had found abandoned in the rear of a repair shop. The bright red paint job I had given it did not conceal the fact that the car needed a lot of work.

The day Sandra took the Fiat, a massive thunderstorm passed over Houston. I was at home and heard a knock on the front door. I opened it and Sandra was standing there, drenched. She had looked beautiful when she left, but her hair had fallen and she was crying. She buried her head in my shoulder and said, "I hate this place." I pulled her inside, dried her off, and assured her everything would be okay. It's one of my fondest memories of our early life together.

She got a job fairly quickly. She had a degree in information management from the business school at San Jose State. She was ahead of the curve.

—

I managed, with a great deal of help, to conduct research and make some important advances in space medicine. One of the first people I met was Judy Hayes, a NASA contractor at the time, who has been with the agency for more than twenty-five years. At the time, she was the only person working in the exercise physiology lab when I came aboard to run it. Judy and I managed to build a pretty substantial program together. In less than a year, we built a twelve- to fifteen-person laboratory. At the time, we were mainly planning the prescriptions and the exercise equipment for space—before the space station had actually happened. The countermeasures we use today are the ones that were developed and defined in 1989 and '90.

After a year I not only headed my own lab, Exercise Physiology, but also was teamed up with four others as part of a larger effort focused on crew health. Our charge was to define the changes that the human body endures because of exposure to microgravity—and to develop countermeasures to prevent them. This involved the development of new medical devices for spaceflight.

The task required the collaboration of the four separate laboratories: exercise physiology, cardiovascular, neuromuscular, and kinesiology. It was a challenge to bring together this disparate group of principal investigators, and I am still proud of our accomplishment today. Our efforts set the foundation for the current health care system on board the International Space Station.

One day I went to one of the heads of the Medical Science Division to inquire about becoming a flight surgeon. I had heard that occasionally NASA would send some of its candidates to the Air Force for special medical training. The assistant director of the division was a medical doctor by the name of Sam Pool. During my tenure within his organization, he provided me lots of advice and guidance about leadership. So, he was very supportive of the idea of me getting additional training.

There were only two places in the country that trained surgeons. One was a civilian program associated with Wright-Patterson Air Force Base in Ohio and the other was in San Antonio at the Brooks Air Force Base at the School of Aerospace Medicine. Most of the NASA docs were sent to Brooks.

Although I had thought about joining the military early in my career, I had decided against it. Now I had the opportunity to join the Air Force through a special program with NASA. In 1989, I was detailed to Brooks as Lieutenant Colonel Harris, the equivalent Air Force rank for my education and experience level.

It was great to be back in San Antonio. The class was made up of about eighty men and women, physicians from different branches of the service, including some foreign military. I was the only civilian. Our classes included many hours of classroom lectures and training in forensic science, survival, and introduction to flight.

As far back as the Revolutionary War, military doctors were referred to as "surgeons," mainly because during battle, surgery was usually required to treat injured soldiers. Much later, during World War I, the airplane was introduced into the battlefield. These new flying machines provided a tremendous advantage to the arena, but they came with a steep human price.

The airplane was a totally different environment, requiring different skills and physical tolerances. As the planes became faster and more agile, flying took a serious physical toll on the crews. We needed to learn more about how the human body responded to flight in order to enhance the pilot's performance. This is where the surgeon's role changed and "flight" was added to the title.

Flight surgeons were initially part of the Army Air Corps, which later became the Air Force. The first were not only trained as doctors; they received flight training too. In order to deal with the issues of human flight, they needed to understand the environment, so they were required to become pilots. At that point, they would speak the language and be respected by the other aviators. As time passed, the role changed again to more of a supporting one, and the requirement for flight training was dropped.

With my basic flight medicine training done, all that was left now was a little course called Introduction to Flight. I remember mine very well. It was at Randolph Air Force Base, in San Antonio, and it was my first ride in a high-performance jet. I had recently completed my private pilot training in Houston, and I had been a newly licensed pilot prior to reporting to Brooks. So I was very excited about the upcoming flight. When we arrived at the student-training center at Randolph, we attended a short ground school followed by a one-hour flight with an instructor. Mine was a very nice guy, but the word was out that most of the instructors saw these flights as an opportunity to strike a blow at flight surgeons all over the world.

Those who are aviators know that the doctors wield a great deal of power when it comes to the flight physical and their ability to ground you. So we were regarded by pilots as both a blessing and a curse. Once we boarded their airplane, however, we became simply "dead meat."

I approached my instructor and greeted him as we both walked toward the plane. It was a T-37, code-named the "Tweet" because when you fired up the engines, it made a characteristic high-pitched noise. It was a two-seater, with the seats side by side so that the instructor could grab the controls and hit you over the head just in case you did something wrong. We got into the jet and—wow!—I was in a real plane. Up until then I had only flown the Cessna 152 and 172, whose top speeds maxed out at a hundred miles per hour, if you had a tailwind.

Suddenly I was at the controls of a high-performance jet with the ability to go more than five hundred miles per hour. We started the plane. It was a little noisy, and I was grateful that I had ear protection. We lined up on the runway, got our clearance, and then we were off. It is hard to describe the feeling of power that you get in a jet. You push the throttle forward, you feel the engines spool up, the plane lunges forward, and within seconds, you are off the ground.

At ten thousand feet over the training range, the pilot began to show me different maneuvers—first a turn to the right, a turn to the left, a short flip upside down, and then back upright. It was fun at first.

"Are you ready for some advanced maneuvers?" he said.

I responded, "Yeah!" That was when things got interesting. He began to climb up to twenty thousand feet and then pushed the nose of the plane over to gain speed. As we gained enough speed, he pulled back sharply on the stick to turn the plane into a 360-degree arc over the top. It was exciting, except for the initial pull-up, which resulted in about 4 Gs along with the sensation that I was being pushed through my seat. (A "G" is your body weight on Earth, so 4 Gs means that you feel like you weigh four times your normal weight.)

I had undergone centrifuge training, and I knew that an M2 maneuver could keep you from fainting. As the tight turns cause an increase in the Gs on the plane and the body, your blood flow shifts from the brain to the feet, resulting in the potential to pass out. The M2 maneuver is a method to increase the blood flow to your brain, by doing straining techniques.

As we went into turn after turn, I was trying to keep up with things by doing the M2, and every time we came out of them, the pilot would turn to me and ask, "Are you all right?"

Each time, I responded, "Great!" But in the back of my mind, I was thinking: *Is this torture ever going to stop? Because I am beginning to not feel so well.* We then went into a "Cuban 8," which is when a pilot noses the plane toward Earth to gain speed, and then pulls up at the last minute, to get the plane to loop over the top, upside down, pulling six to seven Gs. When you get over the top, you flip upright and start the run again in the opposite direction. In the end, you have created a figure eight in the air. It is exciting.

The pilot again asked, "Are you okay?"

"Great!" I said. In truth, I was sick as a dog, but I wasn't going to let him know it. After all, I knew that one of the objectives of the flight was to make as many flight surgeons as sick as possible. I was not going to be one of them—at least not visibly. He soon landed, and I thanked him for the ride and shot him a big thumbs-up. Then I walked very quickly to a spot where no one could see me and threw up. It was a great day after all.

Chapter 5

ONE GIANT LEAP

Your Heart's Desire is the Voice of God,
and that voice must be obeyed sooner or later.
—Emmet Fox

If you are truly driven and motivated to be among the best at what you do, there is always the risk of becoming complacent in your success. I might have been content as a doctor–scientist, punching a clock at the Johnson Space Center. The work was fascinating, a source of quiet discoveries. Or I might have earned an ample and respectable living as a physician in San Antonio, eventually treating the children and grandchildren of my first generation of patients.

But I had been bitten by the astronaut bug. The game had changed since the Original Seven *Mercury* astronauts had kept the country riveted with their solo flights and splashdowns. The change was even more sharply drawn after Neil Armstrong returned from the moon, resisted being a celebrity, and accepted a position on a college faculty, rarely giving an interview. The space shuttle still produced heroes, but the sense of grandeur, adventure, and mystery had waned.

Yet glory or romance were never my needs. At NASA, we were civil servants, government employees, and certainly not in it for the money.

There is a conceit in all this, I know, but I wanted to be tested, to go where so few had gone, to be part of the second age of exploration, like Columbus, Balboa, Magellan, Captain Cook, and others who had charted the unknown and open seas in the first age. Among these other pioneers was the first African-American to explore the Americas: Estevanico, also known as Mustafa Zemmouri, in 1527.

—

In 1989, I had landed back in Houston, the energy capital of the world. Two hundred years younger than New York and Boston, Houston has been described as a small town with a huge population. The ship channel—a fifty-mile ditch that was dug to create a port—and all the Gulf oil made it the tumultuous city it is today. In 1962, when the astronauts arrived, their presence gave breath to what had seemed to many Americans a fantasy: human spaceflight.

The Johnson Space Center had been carved out of rangeland east of Webster and south of Clear Lake, just south of Houston but still within the city's reach. The city spreads at random over the Texas Gulf Plain, flat as a tortilla. The engineers and scientists sent there by their companies tended to stay after the need to stay had passed.

Houston was my home, part of my childhood and college

years, but I had not returned because I wanted a job. I wanted to fly in space! I had spent a couple of years proving myself at NASA, and I was eager to reapply to the astronaut corps. This time I had actual experience working in the space program environment. This round would be different, or so I hoped. I knew that the job I held at the time was a double-edged sword. I would either prove myself or go down in a blaze of defeat. I had to take that chance, so I gave it my all. The call for astronauts went out in late 1989, and I was first in line to apply.

To my surprise I was selected to return for an interview. I knew what to expect. Plus, I was a proven quantity and knew many of the members of the committee, having worked with them in one place or another.

In January 1990, I received the call asking me to show up for astronaut training. I was at Edwards Air Force base as part of the medical team receiving the STS-32 crew, which had been diverted because of foul weather at Cape Canaveral. It was early morning, not long before I was to report for duty; the call came through the base operator. When I answered, Don Puddy, the head of crew flight operations, said, "Bernard, I was just wondering if you wanted that job we talked about earlier this year."

I said, jokingly, "Well, let me think about it for a minute," followed by an emphatic "Yes!"

He told me that I would be receiving an official letter informing me of the details, particularly when and where to show up. When I hung up the phone, I called my parents.

"Guess what?"

They were happy for me, and they spread the word to the rest of the family. That was the only call I could make before having to report to duty for the shuttle landing that morning.

This time as I waited for the shuttle to land, things were different. I was no longer just a scientist or a wannabe astronaut—an "astronaut hopeful," as we were called by the corps. I had become one of the chosen few. The shuttle landed without incident. About an hour later, the crew strolled into the medical facility for the post-flight examination. Commander Dan Brandenstein came up to me with the rest of the crew in tow to say congratulations.

"How did you know?" I asked.

"We were told in orbit yesterday," he said. After all, he was the chief of the Astronaut Office. I was thinking to myself, tongue in cheek, *He could have called.* It was an extremely special and emotional moment for me. I couldn't have dreamed it better.

STS-32 was the thirty-third mission of the space shuttle, whose primary mission was to deploy a navy communications satellite and retrieve the long duration exposure facility, called LDEF. Ironically, the crew included pilot Jim Wetherbee, who would become the commander of my second mission.

Our staff did the staging when people would go out to support these landings. We would send out an early crew to set up and test the equipment to make sure it was working. Later, the rest of the crew would show up, and that night or the next day the shuttle would land. So, when I delivered the news of my selection, our whole team was there, and it was awesome.

In a nice coincidence, Judy Hayes, my colleague from my first days at NASA, was there when the news broke.

Another person who worked with us, David Wolf, who was in life sciences, also had been chosen. We just started celebrating right away. We had a long week out there in the desert, waiting for the shuttle to land, but we enjoyed every minute. It was an incredible experience to be able to share that with them all.

—

In early August 1990, I reported for astronaut training along with twenty-two others from across the country. We were all excited about finally being in the space program. Unlike many of the others, I had already worked for NASA, so I knew some of what to expect, at least the part about working for the government. We had our general orientation followed by the introduction to the media, including group and one-on-one interviews.

It was exciting to be a "real live astronaut," as many people still say to me now when we meet for the first time. Following a tradition that dates back to the very beginning of the program, each class chooses a name for itself. We were the thirteenth group to come into the program, so we named ourselves the "Hairballs." We came up with the moniker because the number thirteen is considered unlucky, as are black cats, and cats cough up hairballs . . . and there you have it. I never said that astronauts were politically correct.

The Hairballs came to know each other well; we were to become a real team. Astronaut candidates are assigned to the

Johnson Space Center in Texas for one year of training and evaluation. Before long we were in classes, learning about things like the geology of the planet and orbital mechanics. We also studied oceanography, astronomy, and engineering, among other subjects. In addition, we were trained to survive in various environments, such as extreme cold and extreme heat, in water and in flight. Our class trained for winter survival in Washington state, but now the classes train for extreme winter survival with the Russians in Siberia. The training was challenging and tough, but for me, it was a labor of love.

We went to the Air Force for jet egress and parachute training. There we learned how to get out of an airplane in case of a catastrophic failure. Later, we had water survival with the Navy in Pensacola, Florida, where we learned how to exit all types of vehicles, boats, helicopters, airplanes, and spaceships, and then had more parachute training.

During this intensive training, we were all acutely aware that in the catastrophic *Challenger* explosion shortly after lift-off in 1986, there had been no escape. All had perished because there was no escape mechanism. Now training is more intense and extensive.

Since so much of the Earth is covered by oceans, the chance of an astronaut ending up in a survival situation in water is more likely than on land. To prepare, we were pushed from boats wearing full packs and helmets to see if we could stay calm and quickly inflate our life jackets. I remember floating around in the Atlantic, wondering if they were ever going to pick us up.

Eventually, we were plucked out of the water to rest a few minutes on a small boat and then pushed right back in. We had thorough training in survival on land, too, thanks to lots of insect appetizers.

One of my favorite parts was the flight training. I already had a private pilot's license and had been exposed to jet aircraft during my flight-surgeon training. This, however, was more comprehensive ground and flight training for the agency's workhorse, the T-38. Flying the jet required a great deal of skill. The aircraft was over thirty years old at the time and had been in the military stable of dependable trainers for many years.

Back then, every Air Force pilot began his or her career flying this airplane. And NASA had used this plane for astronaut flight training since the very beginning of the space program. In the *Apollo* years, the guys used the planes as their personal, cross-country, airborne limo. They didn't exactly have drag races, but they took joyous pride in flying nonstop from Ellington Field, outside of Houston, to Los Angeles, and landing with maybe five to ten minutes' worth of fuel in the tank. They needed a tailwind all the way to make it, but they were supremely confident, and much of that attitude was the result of the one-to-two-year regimen of training they endured. The fear had been trained out of them.

Of course, the T-38 has been upgraded several times in its lifetime. What makes the plane difficult to fly is the very fact that it is aerodynamically unstable, with short wings and very powerful engines. At the same time it is a strong plane, so it takes a lot to destroy it. It's perfect for teaching young pilots how to fly.

I was no different than a lot of young pilots. I was excited to learn how to fly that thing. My first flight was interesting, to say the least. The instructor took off from Ellington Field, heading for the practice range over the Gulf of Mexico, which stretches from the shore of Galveston to New Orleans. When we arrived at altitude, he handed the controls to me to fly straight, maintaining the same altitude. This was one of the most difficult things to learn to do.

As I tried to maintain my altitude, I was making vertical sine waves at thirty thousand feet. At more than four hundred miles per hour, it takes only the slightest movement of the controls to travel up or down a considerable distance, resulting in a dramatic change in altitude. Finally, the instructor said, "Let me take over, because you are making me sick." I was also making myself sick. After a while, though, I got the hang of it. Later, we added the navigation and communication skills to the basic flying.

During training, astronauts have a chance to experience weightlessness. Planes climb up to thirty thousand feet and then dive almost straight down to twenty thousand feet, and then back up again, to simulate microgravity conditions. The passenger seats have been removed, so the astronauts can roll and tumble freely for about thirty seconds in zero gravity, followed by thirty seconds of two times gravity, or two times your normal weight. To create enough free-fall time, you must do about forty parabolas per flight—thus the origin of the nickname, the

"Vomit Comet"—which takes about two hours. At the end of the flight, you received a certificate and a T-shirt if you didn't get sick. I was determined not to give in on my first flight, and I got my shirt. I won't mention what happened on subsequent flights; I'll leave that to your imagination.

We also worked in full-size mock-ups of a space shuttle, containing the onboard systems and payload bay. The simulations, or mock-ups, of problems were so realistic that we felt as if we were actually in the shuttle. At times we would be tilted vertically so the astronauts could experience being on our backs, strapped into our seats as we would be during launch. The entire mission was simulated, from launch to landing. We were given many problems to solve, and we were watched carefully to see how we reacted.

—

After a year of intense study and training, basic training came to an end, and my class graduated. The dream had become a reality. I finally had my silver astronaut pin, awarded for successful completion of the training. The next step was to see if the NASA administrators felt we were ready for a space shuttle assignment.

I would be ready to go after a bit of time off to take a breather and get my bearings. But typically, being assigned to a crew takes quite a while, sometimes years, which is why I thought I might be in trouble when I got a call from the head of the Astronaut Office only three weeks after graduation. They wanted to see me in person, right away.

I was truly worried, and it wasn't a simple case of insecurity. No one grinds his way through the training schedule with perfect scores; there is always a misstep or two. I thought maybe mine had finally occurred.

When I walked into the office, Dan Brandenstein, the chief of the Astronaut Office, said, "Bernard, I have good news and bad news for you."

I smiled and said, "Uh-oh, what'd I do? Better give me the good news first."

"You've been assigned to a mission."

I was immediately so happy, I said, "Wow! You're kidding! That's great! Okay, then what's the bad news?"

"It's a mission with Germany, and you're scheduled to leave in three weeks."

I was blown away. The dream just kept getting better. Not only was I the first person selected from my astronaut class for a space mission, but I would also be part of an international team effort. I would be on the crew of STS-55 *Columbia* that would carry the German D-2 Spacelab into orbit. The mission would be a cooperative effort by the United States, Germany, and eleven other nations that would all contribute to the scientific experiments we would be conducting.

We would train for eighteen months at the German space agency in Cologne, and also have occasional assignments at several other European Space Agency locations. I was at once exhilarated and a little bit scared. To be going to Europe and then into outer space seemed quite a leap, since I had never even been out of my own country. I couldn't wait to get home and tell Sandra: "Guess what! I have some good news and some bad news . . ."

—

After a whirlwind move to Germany, fellow crew member Jerry Ross and I settled into a flat along the Rhine River in Bonn, about fifteen miles from the training center. Jerry was an Air Force colonel who, at that point, had flown on three previous shuttle missions. He was the boss and I was the rookie, and he gave me an education. We became close friends as we trained and lived together in Germany.

To this day, I consider myself fortunate to have worked under such an experienced and enthusiastic professional. Jerry was an engineer from Purdue with Air Force blue running through every vein. He had always wanted to be an astronaut, and he made it his life's work. He has been to space seven times on the shuttle, which makes him the record holder for the most space flights by any astronaut. To honor him, an elementary school was named after him in his hometown of Crown Point, Indiana.

Except for the Americans and the Russians, the Germans have had the most astronauts in space, and they have a training center very similar to ours, complete with simulators and all the rest. They were making their second flight, and Jerry and I were there for payload training in a simulator of the lab we would use on our flight.

For a young man who had not been out of the United States

and hadn't seen too much of the world, it was great duty. From Germany, you can easily reach other European countries by car. We spent many weekends traveling, visiting France, Italy, Switzerland, and Belgium, among other countries. We also happened to be there at a critical moment in German history, just as the Berlin wall was coming down and East and West Germany were reuniting.

When we visited Berlin I was surprised to see how large the wall really was. It cut quite a scar across the city. With the wall coming down, I was proud to know that our international space mission was, in a very direct way, reinforcing the notion that all the walls we construct between countries, creeds, and cultures must eventually crumble, and that peaceful cooperation is really the only way for humankind to fulfill our destiny.

As our planned launch date of March 22, 1993, grew closer, we were told to make sure that our personal affairs were in good order in case of an accident. That may sound kind of morbid, but it is an important part of the business of spaceflight. This precaution requires meeting with the people you love most in the world and planning your own imminent demise. It can be a difficult, painful ordeal. Astronauts don't like it, and families don't like it.

Sandra had recently given birth to our baby daughter, Alexandria, and she was terribly concerned for my safety. Of course, just two years prior to my entering the astronaut program, she and I, like most Americans, had experienced the nationally televised pain of the *Challenger* disaster; we had no delusions about the dangers of spaceflight.

I personally regard every space mission as a near-death experience requiring mental preparation, not very different from that of a soldier going off to war. So, when it neared the time for my first flight, I put my important papers into my "death folder," had several heartfelt and loving conversations with Sandra and other loved ones, and headed to Florida. There, family and friends soon gathered at the Kennedy Space Center for the launch. Many of them had tried to persuade me along the way that flying in space was too dangerous. But I have always believed that going for what you want in life is worth the risk. And more important, I would rather die attempting to fulfill a dream than sitting on the sidelines in fear.

And so it was that, on the appointed day, I found myself strapped in tightly 150 feet above the ground along with my six fellow travelers, all of us sitting on top of enough rocket fuel to lift 5 million pounds into Earth orbit. One side of my brain was thinking, *This is great. I'm going to launch into space today*, and the other side was thinking, *What in the world am I doing here?*

But things were looking good. I was there with my buddy, Jerry Ross, and the rest of the crew. I had the utmost confidence in our mission commander, Steve Nagel, one of the most experienced, personable, terrific guys I had ever worked with. I was trained. I was focused. I was in the moment. I was ready. The countdown was proceeding flawlessly. We heard the main engine start . . . and then all hell broke loose—or *didn't* break loose, which is thankfully a lot closer to what happened.

Just seconds after the main engines ignited, the computer

controlling the launch sequence suddenly shut them down, and the whole ship started rocking.

The Space Transportation System, or STS, more commonly known as the space shuttle, is an assembly of four major components: the shuttle vehicle, two solid rocket boosters, and a huge main fuel tank. The shuttle vehicle has three main engines on the back. When this whole "stack" of components is assembled prior to launch, it stands up vertically on the launching pad, where it is held in place by four huge bolts on the skirts of the solid rocket boosters.

When the stack is standing vertically, it is delicately balanced, with the center of gravity on the side where the shuttle is mounted. In order for the liftoff to be smooth, the computer first lights the three main engines on the shuttle side, creating one and a half million pounds of thrust. However, at this point there is no counterbalancing thrust coming off the solid rocket engines on the other side. So that initial thrust from the shuttle's main engines pushes the whole stack a bit off its vertical alignment by about ten to fifteen feet, and then it "twangs" (not to be confused with Tang) back toward vertical again. That takes about five seconds, and just as the stack reaches the correct vertical position again, the computer lights the two solid rocket boosters and releases the four bolts that hold everything down. Then the vehicle lifts off on a perfect vertical, as it's supposed to do.

The shuttle sequence is different now from that of the *Apollo* era, when they made sure that all the engines were running and then released the bolts. If an engine failed at that point, they could actually terminate before releasing the bolts.

This is all very tricky rocket science, worked out carefully in advance by physicists and mathematicians who eat this stuff for breakfast.

But what happened in our sequence was this: Columbia was still on the launching pad, we were buckled into our seats, and there was this Niagara Falls type of noise from the sound suppression system. Then suddenly the countdown was halted, and there was only the sensation of the rocket moving—the twang—as Jerry Ross said, "Are we moving?"

None of us had seen this before. We had heard about it, but there was no way to simulate it in our training. Visualize looking through a porthole and seeing and feeling the whole world outside swaying back and forth, and you'll have an idea of what we experienced.

Throughout this wild, disorienting action, as I watched things move sideways, I was just sitting there thinking, *Please God, let those bolts hold!* And then the master alarm went off in my ear. As a result of our training, no one said what we were all thinking—"Oh, shit, are we about to blow?" I could actually hear the control center say, "Launch pad abort." This was at T minus three seconds. In the control room they were flipping through the launch pad abort pages, and we could hear them as they rattled off the checklist for the state of the vehicle: "So and so, check; so and so, check."

At that point, I was sitting on the flight deck, and I had the window behind me; I was looking through the wrist mirror on my suit. I could see where the engines had fired and how smoke was billowing. That's when my training kicked in again. I started looking for options out of the situation. Option A was to jump. But we were 150 feet in the air, the rocket was swaying back and forth fifteen feet, and as part of the abort procedure, we had to leave our parachutes, so forget that. Option B was to try to reach the gantry arm that swung over us, but the gantry arm was out of reach, and if we tried to jump, the least of the injuries would be a broken back.

Suddenly we heard a call for a crew escape, which meant they had to bring the gantry back. One by one we headed for the hatch, and the gantry team was at the door, ready to help us. There was at least a foot-and-a-half gap we had to step over, in our heavy, bulky suits, and two technicians were straddling the gap to help us get across to safety.

Of course, the launches are suspenseful and tense and exhausting without any added attractions. But on this particular day, as the computer was monitoring the operation of the main engines, it detected a flaw in the tip-seal retainers of the turbo pumps. So it shut the engines down after only a couple of seconds. When the computers detected an incomplete ignition, the abort message was sent. That meant the stack initially rocked off its vertical axis as planned, but then when it twanged back, the solid rocket motors did not light. The shuttle's main engines were off, we didn't launch, and we therefore had to wait for the twanging to dampen out. Fortunately, it did, with the bolts holding fast.

We had survived a last minute pad abort and a liberal dose of twang. We were relieved, but we didn't have the luxury of feeling that we had cheated death. While we had lived to fly another day, our disappointment was strong, and we worried about whether we had lost our opportunity.

This experience had taught me many lessons. When launch day was close, my family and friends gathered in Florida to watch with both pride and fear. They all prayed that everything would go well, even though they knew I was doing what I wanted to do, whatever the outcome. I was sorely disappointed again by the delays and did my share of griping. But those delays actually helped my family to mentally prepare for the actual launch. The family had not been ready to let me go. Waiting a month and seeing all the extra procedures and care NASA took to find the problems, they felt confident that everything would be all right. I had not seen this from my vantage point. All I could see was the disappointment, my childhood dream on the verge of being dashed.

Sometimes our dreams conflict with those of the people around us. If dreams are to be, then they will be, at the right time—a time that best serves all involved. We are sometimes selfish creatures, thinking only of our own needs and desires. But if we are open to the world around us, we eventually discover the things that are truly ours.

Chapter 6

AROUND THE WORLD

Success is not measured by what a man accomplishes, but by the
opposition he has encountered and the courage with which he has
maintained the struggle against overwhelming odds.
—Charles Lindbergh

After the failed launch, the crew and I were very disappointed to say the least. We thought that we would be in space doing our jobs. Instead we had to wait.

I would argue that waiting for a spaceflight ranks near the top of the list of the hardest things I have had to do. The wait for the launch of STS-55 was nearly unbearable. The seven of us who comprised the crew for this space shuttle, the fourteenth flight of *Columbia*, thought the day could not come soon enough. We were fretful because we knew that anything could happen, and the flaws that may postpone a launch, no matter how minor or easily fixed, cause foreboding. It is a mind-set we tried to avoid at all cost. It didn't help when I would get questions from friends and the media about the risk of spaceflight: "Aren't you concerned about dying?" My answer was simple: I would rather die doing what I love than to live in a state of fear and regret.

Our liftoff was delayed *four* times. That may not be the record, but it was three more than we had hoped for. *Columbia* was initially scheduled to launch as early as February 1993, but the date had slipped to early March due to concerns over the tip-seal containers in the turbo pumps in the main engines. All three pumps were replaced at the pad, and a later inspection revealed that the retainers were in good condition.

Then a hydraulic flex hose burst in the aft compartment during the Flight Readiness Test. The lines were removed and inspected and replaced. The launch was rescheduled for March 22 and, as described earlier, was aborted three seconds before liftoff. A month passed while the technicians replaced all the main engines, and the engineers parsed all the data and checked every nook and cranny.

Another attempt was scrubbed on April 24 due to a possible faulty reading with one of the inertial measurement units. Finally, on April 26, 1993, after an exhaustive inspection of component parts and a final, thorough investigation of everything that happened during our aborted launch, NASA again pronounced the ship ready to go. This time the system worked flawlessly, and the mission was everything I had hoped it would be.

—

Here's just a taste of what we experienced: As you lie on your back waiting to blast off, there is a lot of time to think about what you are about to do. In your head, you think about your family and friends and all the things you've left undone. You wonder whether this will be your final ride. Then you are shocked back into reality by the closing countdown: T minus ten seconds . . . five, four, three, two, one, liftoff!

When the shuttle lifts off the pad, it looks very slow and stately from a distance. But for a passenger, the ride is pretty wild. The vehicle is kicked into space with 7.5 million pounds of thrust from all the engines. There is incredible noise and vibration, and a pressure that feels almost like someone is sitting on your chest.

Shortly after clearing the launch pad, you are already approaching the sound barrier at more than seven hundred miles per hour. Within two minutes you are a hundred thousand feet above the Earth, nearly twenty miles high and traveling at a speed of twenty-five hundred miles per hour. At that point, the solid rocket boosters are released. As these boosters fall back toward Earth, parachutes deploy to slowly lower them into the ocean for recovery.

Now you are above most of the atmosphere, so there is nothing holding you back. The spaceship continues to accelerate to 18,000 miles per hour over the next 6.5 minutes, as the G load on the crew increases to 3–3.5 times their weight. At this point, breathing is no longer involuntary. You must tell yourself to breathe every few seconds.

Once you are safely in space, the main engine cuts off, and the big external fuel tank that has been supplying the three main shuttle engines is jettisoned. It falls back into the atmosphere and burns up on its way to the Pacific Ocean. Then the shuttle is in orbit, and you go from being pushed back in your seat from the pressure of pulling 3 Gs, to immediately weightless in a split second. Suddenly everything is floating, including you. And all that happens in just 8.5 minutes!

The view is truly magnificent. Attempts to describe this sight have led generations of astronauts to wish for a poet onboard to do justice to this vision. The reality is that not many could survive the rigors of the training, much less the flight. But the sheer beauty is, indeed, in the eye of the beholder: There are arrays of colors, rainbows, twinkling city lights at night, lightning flashes in the tops of clouds, and a marvelous view of the continents.

—

The science on STS-55 was as fascinating as the view. We worked in two shifts around the clock to complete investigations into the areas of fluid physics, material sciences, life sciences, biological sciences, technology, Earth observations, atmospheric physics, and astronomy. As the crew medical officer and mission specialist, my job was to ensure the health of the team and to conduct scientific investigations.

At one point, I did an echocardiogram of my own heart and looked at it on a screen. The heart actually shrinks in size and shifts in the chest during weightless conditions. I used my stethoscope to listen for heart sounds, and I discovered I had to listen in a slightly different place than I did when on Earth.

We also performed a cell fusion in microgravity much more

efficiently than we could have on earth, fusing two types of white blood cells to create a hybrid cell that could make antibodies against viral diseases. And we performed the first intravenous saline injection in space, to help us study body fluid replacement after prolonged weightlessness.

In all, we performed eighty-eight experiments originating from eleven nations, most of them aimed at furthering our understanding of the effects of space travel on the human body. We also worked in the SpaceHab module, which fits into the payload bay, an area large enough to hold a semi truck and trailer.

In general, most astronauts lose five to ten pounds per mission due to several causes, such as loss of fluid, muscle, and bone. In fact, on a typical mission, astronauts lose 1 percent of our bone density per month, one-fifth of our blood volume, and 10 to 15 percent of our muscle mass.

The bone marrow makes less blood, too, so anemia is a problem after a few months in space. Most astronauts also experience space motion sickness for a few days until the brain adjusts to the mixed signals it experienced in microgravity. All this information is important for the doctors who practice medicine in space.

The mission of STS-55 was an inspiring, exhilarating, exhausting ten days in space, during which we flew more than four million miles. For me, the flight had been a life-changing experience. But an even better one was yet to come, almost two years later.

—

February 9, 1995 was a record-breaking day at the apex of an historic flight that began on February 3. Three firsts, described earlier, were written on the stars—Eileen Collins as the first female pilot; Michael Foale as the first British astronaut to fly in space; and I, the first African-American to walk in space. And then we accomplished yet another first by moving a satellite around by hand. Plus, Mike and I felt we had prevailed simply by not becoming the first astronauts to freeze our tassels off in space.

On this, my second flight, I had moved up to payload commander. Ironically, the little boy who was forced to use the back door of a diner in the sixties because of his race had triumphed in the nineties. It was my day, and I was flying very high!

As Mike and I completed our duties and stowed the satellite safely into the cargo bay for the trip home, I felt a rush of emotions. I had set this goal so many years ago, and I had reached it. At the same time, I had pushed aside another barrier and opened the doors of space even wider to men and women of all races.

During our spacewalk, I had the opportunity to relax through a full day and night pass. I dangled from the robotic arm, about thirty-five feet above the payload bay, looking down at my fellow crew members in the ship. Behind them was the enormous planet Earth, and beyond that, the rest of the universe.

I felt extremely small in comparison to the grand scheme of things. Who wouldn't? But for an instant, a speck of sand in the hourglass of time, I became larger than life. This was when the realization kicked in that I was one of a handful, among billions of humans, who had actually flown into space, let alone walked in space!

The lesson is simple and pure: Remember how important dreams are. The greatest loss of all is that many of us never fulfill our dreams, our ambitions, our hopes. This may be a result of our environment, our background, our fears, or the fact that we simply give up. In my opinion, this is a loss not only for the individual but for all of us, because our world can never benefit from all of those unfulfilled dreams.

One of my favorite authors is the contemporary philosopher and spiritual teacher Eckhart Tolle. His book *The Power of Now* made a lasting impression on me. His most basic teaching is, I believe, something everyone—and certainly every astronaut—could use to improve their daily lives and their ability to achieve success, particularly when facing complex, daunting endeavors: Live in the present.

Remember that the past is over and done. The future has not yet happened, and it is certainly not under your control. All you have, and all you will *ever* have, is the moment you are living *right now*.

This quote from *The Power of Now* may drive the point home:

Accept—then act. Whatever the present moment contains, accept it as if you had chosen it. Always work with it, not against it. Make it your friend and ally, not your enemy. This will miraculously transform your whole life.

When I was in space, alone, absorbing the essence of the universe around me, I was in the awe-inspiring moment. There was no past or future. All daily living, whether it is conducting a business meeting, driving your car from your home to your job, managing your personal finances, even surviving the cold in outer space, is about accepting what happens at any given moment and working with it to produce the best outcome.

If you're late because you're stuck in a traffic jam, relax, listen to music or the news, call your appointment and reschedule, smile, sing your favorite song out loud, and remind yourself how good it is to be alive at that moment.

When you learn to react to adversity by always accepting it and then moving forward—forward toward a solution—you will never get "stuck" in a loop of self-defeating fear and pain.

Does being present mean that we should never learn from or honor the past? Of course not. It simply means that right *now*, in this moment, we should focus on the task at hand. Does being in the present mean that we should not plan for the future? Certainly not. It simply means that we are choosing this moment to do that planning, and we should do it to the best of our abilities, just as an astronaut would focus on a difficult training exercise to prepare for a future spaceflight.

At times, when I feel a special need, I repeat this small affirmation to myself:

Just for today I will not fear. I will be unafraid to enjoy the possessions I have gained from my success. I will be unafraid to enjoy the beauty around me. I will be unafraid to believe in the people in my life and the possibilities of the world. Just for today I will let go of the past, focus on the present, and positively await the future.

Let's face it. Achievement is never easy. It takes hard work. In order to achieve, you must have a level of clarity about your goals. And when I have achieved in my life, in college, in medicine, in NASA, in business, I have been in the *moment.* Some people call it "being in the flow." Great athletes like Michael Jordan or Tiger Woods refer to something they call the "zone." It is that mindless state when all the endless background noise in your head magically disappears, when your doubts and fears melt away. Confidence reigns supreme and you are totally focused on the task at hand. It is *learned* behavior—not something that happens by accident—and it starts with living in the present.

At one time or another, each of us should have a chance to spread our wings. You need not be a superstar. When our daughter was younger, I took her to see the movie *Space Jam,* in which Michael Jordan plays a basketball player who overcame obstacles to soar above the competition. When we find our place in this world, when we discover our abilities and believe in ourselves, we obtain our wings to fly—in life. My favorite song from that same movie is "I believe I can fly."

—

After the mission, the crew flew home from Cape Canaveral in Florida. There is a tradition that after each spaceflight, the crew returns to Houston for a huge celebration, where NASA employees who have worked on the mission and other space supporters gather to welcome us home. These are wonderful events. We land, wave to the crowd, and give speeches in our own words about the mission and our appreciation of the efforts of the people on the ground.

I felt then, and I still feel, truly appreciative of the many who came before who laid the foundation for me, and those who tirelessly worked so many hours to ensure that we had a successful flight.

It is a tradition for the local sheriff's department to escort each crew member home, sirens blasting through the streets in celebration of our safe return to Earth. On the way home from my last mission, Sandra and I were alone in the backseat of the car. I remember leaning over to her and saying, "Honey, I think this will be my last flight."

She looked at me, smiled, and said, "You're just saying that because you're tired." Indeed I was. It had taken more than twenty-five years to get there, from the first lunar landing and my declaration that I would become an astronaut. Then came the years of training and effort to accomplish something that few people ever do. Yes, I was weary from the nine-day mission to *Mir* and the forty-five experiments that we had just completed. But I didn't need rest; I needed a new direction.

After a terrific although challenging time at NASA, I

suddenly realized it was time to leave. Everyone always says you should leave at the top of your game, and I did. During a decade at NASA, I'd had a successful research career as a clinical scientist, become a NASA flight surgeon through training with the Air Force, and participated as an astronaut on two spaceflight missions. I had served as the chief medical officer and payload commander, not to mention conducting a spacewalk. But more important, I had accomplished all my childhood dreams. Many people would be envious of such a run; I was simply grateful to have had the opportunity.

In 1995, I was approached by a senior manager of one of the NASA contractors, inquiring if I was ready to leave the agency. He didn't know of my recent conversation with my wife about leaving. Many months later the manager made good on his promise to get back to me, and he offered me a job. I accepted it.

The time had come to move on. I was mentally and emotionally ready to leave, and I was also ready to strive for another of my goals: to make a transition to the world of business and finance. I would explore a new career and truly learn the meaning of a word that sounded somewhat fancy for a kid from the West End in Houston and the Navajo reservations of Arizona and New Mexico; I was ready to turn my sights on being an *entrepreneur.*

Chapter 7

A Capital Idea

Success is never final. Failure is never fatal.
Courage is what counts.
—Sir Winston Churchill

I don't know of any astronauts who retired when they turned sixty-five, collecting their pension and maybe a gold watch and riding off into the sunset.

Once an astronaut has felt that rush of orbiting Earth and returning alive, there is no easy transition to anything else. It's difficult for a former astronaut to imagine successfully meeting a comparable challenge. A few have stayed the course at NASA, going into management. Maybe half a dozen former astronauts have held political office, notably John Glenn, elected to the U.S. Senate from Ohio and once a candidate for president. Some found that their experience was valued on the boards of corporations, and others became consultants to space contractors. Many have found jobs as engineers or earned a living on the lecture circuit.

Frank Borman was high-profile as the president of Eastern Airlines, and the late Alan Shepard flourished in banking and real estate. But not many others, if any, struck it rich in business, big or small.

When I decided to become an entrepreneur, I wasn't trying to break new ground. I only wanted to heed the advice of my childhood friend, Cleverick, to think bigger. Cleverick went on to become a successful dentist, and I'm guessing he invested well. I have no idea if he reached his goal of making $10 million.

In April 1996, fourteen months after my flight on the space shuttle *Discovery*, I joined SpaceHab, an aerospace company backed by venture capital. The company believed, as I did, that the industry would evolve to the point where private companies would play a more critical role in space exploration. Many of my friends and associates thought I was crazy to leave NASA after such a productive career. But change in life is certain, and I was ready for a change.

I negotiated a position as a vice president, reporting directly to the company's CEO. My job was to assist in creating new opportunities for the company, outside of the contract it already had with NASA. I would be developing business for customers interested in flying commercial payloads and experiments in space. SpaceHab had invested in the development of a laboratory that fit inside the cargo bay of the shuttle, as on my second spaceflight. It was a module that could be outfitted with different experiments tailored to the specifications of the customer. The company had a contract with NASA to fly the module, and we sold opportunities to our clients for them to perform their experiments in space.

During the year and a half I was the vice president of Life Sciences, I brought a number of new ideas to the company for consideration. One of those was to get the company into commercial markets outside of the space industry, but where they could use their expertise. I pulled together a team and began to form strategic partnerships with some of the other leading companies in the aerospace industry. The products and services proposal was to start with automatic defibrillators on airlines, to create a device capable of providing in-flight medical care utilizing telecommunications (telemedicine). The project was going well, and the company management appeared interested, until the final stages of the deal, when it all fell apart.

The CEO and other senior managers began to raise more and more questions, making it difficult for the deal to survive. There was only one set of marbles for all the senior management team to play with, so we had to constantly compete with one another. I found out that not everyone played fairly and that some people will actively seek your destruction for personal gain. I was being outmaneuvered at every turn. It shook my confidence, and as the deal fell apart, so did I.

I eventually recovered, and I developed a plan to turn my lemons into lemonade. First, I took myself out of the battle for power within the company. I realized that, despite my considerable education up to that point, none of it had provided me with expertise for business. I needed to gain more knowledge about business as fast as possible. The only way I knew to do this was through formal education. Which meant that I needed to go back to school.

I happened to have been in a board meeting a few days earlier, when a colleague mentioned a new MBA program for physicians at the University of Houston at Clear Lake. I convinced the CEO of SpaceHab to support my attending the university to obtain a master of business administration. That schooling helped me realize that I would never thrive at SpaceHab. I had learned a great deal, particularly about corporate culture—and why I had taken such a fall earlier in my time with the company. In retrospect, it was probably the best thing that could have happened to me at the time. I made my decision; it was time to go.

Just as I was preparing to leave, the company decided to start a new entity called Space Media, and I was asked to step in as vice president of business development. It looked like a great opportunity to get away from the aerospace business and into the new Internet technology. Investors were pouring money into Internet-related businesses during this period. At the same time, we proposed a space-based platform to create content in space that could be delivered in a variety of ways, including via the Internet.

Everyone thought it was a great plan. In the midst of creating Space Media, however, the Internet bubble burst and so did the fledgling company. I was suddenly forced to find a different path.

—

Since the first time that I heard the words "venture capital," I have been fascinated by the idea of becoming an entrepreneur and investing in advanced technology and high-growth companies. One day I was having breakfast with a friend who had been in venture capital for many years. I told him of my interest in intelligent funding of high-potential companies and asked how I could break into the business. He promptly told me that you cannot break into venture capital; you must be invited. His words put into perspective the challenge ahead of me.

Shortly afterward, I was invited to speak at a conference of thoracic surgeons in San Diego, California. By chance, I was on the dais with Dr. Jack Gill, cofounder and managing partner of Vanguard Ventures. And, as often had occurred at critical stages in my life, fate intervened. I learned that Jack Gill began his venture capital career during the early days in Silicon Valley in the seventies. He grew his firm into a multimillion-dollar empire with eight successful funds over the course of twenty-five years. When I saw what he had done, I knew I had found not only a business model but a role model.

Jack didn't know me, but we had mutual friends in the medical community—doctors—and one of them was Dr. Julie Swain, one of the few female heart surgeons in America. For some time, she had been urging me to go meet this guy, knowing he spent part of his time in Texas. Here we were a year or two later; Jack and I were back-to-back keynote speakers at the conference. He gave a wonderful talk on investing in health care. I was engrossed in everything that he had to say.

So, I followed him. We said hello for the first time as he left the podium. Jack told me later that he was impressed by me, and he went out of his way to get to know me better. Truth be told, I was more than interested in getting to know him, too. Three hours later, we happened to meet at the front curb of the hotel and shared a cab to the airport. I told him about my medical career and spaceflights. A couple of months later I went to see him. I was ready to move on from SpaceHab, my first dabble in the business world.

We talked, and he advised me: "Bernard, with all due respect for all your space achievements and medical success, I don't see any business experience on your résumé, and people will treat you differently until you have some."

I listened closely as he told me what kind of experience would be valuable. He said, "If you want a shortcut, go get an MBA, and if you add that on top of your MD and NASA career, no one can say you don't have any business credentials."

I proudly informed him that I was in the process of completing an MBA.

Meeting Jack Gill enabled me to turn the corner in my decision to move into the venture capital business and to begin a lifelong friendship. He was willing to share his experience and encouraged me, even placing me on the boards of a couple of his portfolio companies. This allowed me to get true experience in the industry at its roots.

In 2001, after looking over the shoulders of Jack and his partners, in particular Dr. Bob Ulrich, I was convinced that venture capital should be my next profession. I persuaded Vanguard Ventures to be the lead for the creation of a new company that would focus on the futuristic world of telemedicine. I wanted a name that was related to health care and had historical significance, and I ended up naming the company Vesalius Ventures, after Andrea Vesalius, a sixteenth-century Belgian physician who is considered by many to be the father of modern medicine.

A year later, Vesalius was formed. With Jack's firm as the lead investor, I managed to recruit two other firms, Guidant Corporation and Fremont Ventures, to join the investor group. The business model was not new. The industry had been combining interested venture capital firms and corporations for quite some time. These were called "incubators," and Vanguard had created many of them over the years to explore opportunities in different markets.

I learned my lessons about running a business and making investments through trial and error. One lesson is the importance of integrity, and a second is the willingness to work hard. I have always heard that nothing worthwhile is ever easy. During my tenure as a venture capitalist, nothing could have been more true. My entry into this world was difficult, highlighted by the fact that I had no experience in private equity financing and only limited experience as a businessman. Of course, I had managed multimillion-dollar programs for the government and served as a senior manager for private corporations, but nothing prepared me for the world that I had entered.

I had seen venture capitalists from the outside looking in, and I was amazed by the wealth being built by the few, not to mention the impact they were making on the economy. What I did not really understand was what it took to break into the business. Venture capital is the tip of the spear when it comes to building individual wealth, and there are only a handful of people who make it to the top.

Most of those who get there do not want to share the pie. It is a high-risk, high-reward industry, where only a very few deals create great returns that make up for all the failures. You succeed only if you are lucky or blessed.

One of those willing to share his experience and assist in my education was Jack's partner, Bob Ulrich. With his guidance, over time Vesalius has undergone somewhat of an evolution, and it's a different entity than when we started. I was initially supported as a talent scout to make contacts and see all the things that were going on in the world of telemedicine.

Vesalius was located in Houston, because we were of the opinion that this city, home of the world's largest medical center, was a potentially lucrative area. If you look at how many research dollars flow into Texas, and then you look at the amount of commercial investment that results from that and compare it to Silicon Valley and Boston, you can see the obvious opportunity.

One of the other things that became obvious as I learned more about the venture capital industry is that there were not many minorities or women in the business. I saw the same demographic at every firm I visited: white middle-aged men. Finally, I found an organization, National Association of Investment Companies (NAIC), that focuses on minorities and women in the private equity industry. I recall going to my first NAIC conference and finally feeling that I was not alone. The NAIC also gave me a place to seek advice from peers who were already successful in the business, providing me with a great networking opportunity.

—

One of the things that I love most about this new life is the opportunity to assist entrepreneurs with novel ideas that positively impact our world. These people are young at heart, whatever their age. They arrive with the imagination and energy of a child, driven by their passion to bring their ideas to the marketplace. In many cases the only thing that prevents this from happening is the lack of money to fund the creation of the company, and the lack of knowledge to avoid the pitfalls that every entrepreneur encounters when bringing a new product or service to market. My job is to assist in this process. It is the challenge that gets me up in the morning.

Within months after closing my financing for Vesalius, we had a great deal on the table. The entrepreneur was looking for financing, the technology was novel, and the application was groundbreaking. We worked for months with the fledgling company and our investors to fund the deal.

In the venture capital business, investments are made with successive rounds of funding: The earliest is the "seed" stage, and subsequent rounds usually are designated as Series A, Series B, Series C, and so forth. At each stage the investments get larger, requiring more investors to be added to the mix. At some point, when the company has customers and is earning significant revenue, it is ready for an "exit." The exit is the point at which the investors either look for a way to sell the company through a merger or acquisition, or recapitalize it through an initial public stock offering (an IPO).

In this case, I managed to convince the investors to commit to a $5 million seed investment in the company, and all was right with the world. There was just one thing standing in the way—the founder of the company. The same entrepreneur with whom I had been working all along decided to change the deal and attempt to play the investors against one another in order to raise his profile and the terms of the deal.

This spooked the investors by raising questions about the trustworthiness of the founder. As a rule, when you fund business opportunities, you are in fact investing in the people of the company. Investors will not put money into people they do not trust. The founder's actions caused mistrust in the relationship, and suddenly the deal was dead.

I was offended by his lack of integrity. He wanted to cut us out of the picture. But the investors needed us to monitor the company's progress.

This was my first deal and my first lesson in venture capital.

It was a very painful lesson to learn after spending months working on the deal. My partner, a seasoned venture capitalist, had seen founders behave this way many times before. Sometimes founders get too greedy and/or are afraid to let go, so they do things that limit, and in some cases destroy, the very opportunity that they want. My partner called it "founderitis."

I have been involved with many deals since then, and I have learned many more lessons. During the course of reviewing hundreds of deals, I have developed a great volume of experience with entrepreneurs, advanced technology, and simple human nature. In the investment business you cannot ignore the tendency of people to be themselves. I have learned to take this into account on every deal that I am involved with. I have had to become creative in order to get the deal done. As a consequence, I have expanded the incubator model to include companies with existing technology. Some of these are large corporations that want to offer their products and services to the health care industry. We have now done this successfully on several occasions.

Putting it all together as an entrepreneur and venture capitalist required me to create an organization by finding the right people, those who share my values. When it came to raising capital for the firm, I had to convince others to trust *me* with their money.

During my years at the helm of Vesalius Ventures, I have also witnessed the evolution of the health care industry, in which technology has extended the provider's ability to serve the needs of patients more efficiently and effectively. I believe that, when fully realized, the application of telemedicine technologies will completely transform health care as we now know it.

After eight years in the venture capital business, Vesalius has been involved in funding a number of successful companies, building wealth, creating jobs, and setting the stage for the creation of our first venture capital fund.

—

I am keenly aware of my debt to Jack Gill. He not only advised and supported me, but also waged a one-man campaign to have me inducted into the Horatio Alger Association of Distinguished Americans.

Horatio Alger, Jr., was a nineteenth-century American who was an astute observer of the early pioneers and entrepreneurs in this country. He wrote some 155 books about them and became a famous author living mainly in Boston and New York for most of his life. He died in 1899. His books were widely read and in the public eye for another twenty to thirty years, but then his work was mostly forgotten and passed into history.

Then in 1947 the famous author and minister Norman Vincent Peale cofounded the Horatio Alger Association of Distinguished Americans with educator Kenneth Beebe to resurrect the legacy of Alger's work. The purpose was to select about ten entrepreneurs every year using three criteria. Inductees must (1) overcome great adversity in growing up; (2) go on to rise above that and become big successes; and (3) not forget their roots, and give back through philanthropy, volunteerism, and helping others.

Every year two thousand names are talked about, and a process narrows that list down to a few hundred, and then the Horatio Alger Association board of directors nominates the finalists. There is great diversity among honorees who include presidents, senators, aviators, astronauts, pioneers, actors, actresses, entertainment and sports figures, great intellects, academics, doctors, and pioneering American businesspeople.

About six hundred members have been elected in about sixty years. Of those about three hundred are still living. When you look at the list, you see the great company that members are in—big names like the founders of Wal-Mart, IBM, American Airlines, and Starbucks. Among the aviators are generals Jimmy Doolittle and Chuck Yeager and astronaut Buzz Aldrin.

In 1999, Jack nominated me for the Horatio Alger Award. Usually so many people are nominated, so many great names, it takes three to five years for a person to get vetted, meet some of the other members, and make the cut. Jack believes that I may be one of the few candidates who was picked the first time nominated.

I will be eternally grateful to him for his efforts in promoting me for this unique honor.

Bernard as a medical student talking to an elementary class in Lubbock, TX

Bernard, Rex Mann, and Michael Robertson at graduation from Texas Tech University School of Medicine, Lubbock, TX

Bernard in the front seat of the T-38

Bernard's astronaut photo

Bernard's first ride on the KC-135, Zero-G airplane
(the "Vomit Comet")

Floating with Judy Hayes in zero gravity on the KC-135 airplane

STS-55 mission patch

The STS-55 crew

STS-55 crew at Kennedy Space Center during "Dry Count,"
the practice launch

Sandra and Bernard at a speaking event in Lubbock, TX,
following the first space shuttle mission

Bernard in a Launch Entry Suit (LES)

STS-63 mission patch

The STS-63 crew

ASTRONAUT BERNARD HARRIS: THE NEWEST CHAPTER

Cartoon that ran in the San Antonio Express-News *during Black History Month.*

Bernard during EVA (Extravehicular Activity), looking back at the cargo bay of the shuttle

Bernard and Mike hanging in space

Bernard during EVA, with "Guns Up" for Texas Tech University

Mike and Bernard in airlock before going outside

Bernard and Mike working in the cargo bay of Discovery

STS-63 crew meets President Clinton

Bernard holding an Educational Forum in Mobile, AL

Bernard and two students during a description of
liftoff at the DREAM Tour

Bernard, Sandra, and Alex

Alex at the Holiday Parade in Houston, TX, 2009

Joe and Gussie Burgess, Bernard's parents

Bernard's sister, Gillette, and mother, Gussie, at the mall

Chapter 8

GIVING BACK, PAYING FORWARD

*There is no greater joy nor greater reward than to make
a fundamental difference in someone's life.*
—Henry Moore

My grandmother Mary said that when I was born, I lay in the crib with my hand open. This meant, according to country lore, that I would be a "giver."

She reminded me of this from time to time, when she saw me sharing my candy or toys or listening to strangers. She described me as "free-hearted," someone who is always looking for a way to help people. "You should be careful that you don't give everything away," she would caution.

I would simply roll my eyes, as little boys tend to do, and dismiss her as a sweet old lady with concerns for her grandson. I always wondered how she could know what was in my heart. But as I grew older, I discovered that there was some truth in her words. I am a giver and a caregiver. When it comes to giving back, I feel I have no choice; it's part of my DNA. It's also been part of any success I've had.

My great-grandmother, the one we called Honey, always said that no matter how hard you try, "You can't take it with you." She meant that the riches of this world, which we all strive to amass, will remain on Earth after we die. I hate to put it so bluntly, but on this point there is no debate.

Many have written about this in many different cultures and religions. There is something about believing that is ingrained in our core as human beings.

My beliefs align with what the Bible says about giving: You must give in order to receive. I believe that a large part of success comes through giving, and each of us must give back in our own way. This means that in addition to donating money, we can donate our time, attention, knowledge, and love.

There is no one method of giving back. There is no certain amount of money or time that must be given. We should simply give of ourselves no matter what. Whatever your belief may be, in order to obtain and maintain, you must give back what has been given to you. (*Obtaining* means acquiring things in life that we need and/or desire, and *maintaining* means holding on to what we have.)

When giving, you run the risk that what you give will not flow back to you. If this happens, however, what you have given will not be lost; someone will reap the benefit of your generosity.

Our legacy is the only thing we leave behind when we depart this world. If that legacy has come about through helping those around us, then we will have truly lived a good life. I choose to draw from all my resources when giving back. By resources

I mean time, money, skills, knowledge, and influence, which I can use to make a difference. In 1998 I established a foundation as a means to give back. The Harris Foundation supports educational programs throughout the United States. Our passion is education, which encourages and enables dreams as nothing else can. You remember the famous saying: "Buy a man a fish, and you feed him for a day. Teach a man to fish, and you feed him for life." By expanding an individual's knowledge, you can enable him to become a fisherman in life.

This wisdom has always been a part of my life, so it plays an important role in the way I give back. Another famous saying, or principle, is "Pay it forward"; it means that when people help you in some way, instead of repaying them, you show kindness to the next person. By giving to the next person, you help create a chain of giving that moves forward and multiplies at each encounter.

Why is giving important to me? The answer is basic: My achievements came on the shoulders of those who blazed a trail before me and those who extended a hand all along the way. I had no choice but to do the same for those around me. No man is an island; no man can stand alone in a storm without others to hold him steady.

Another law of giving is that it never happens in a vacuum. The things that we do—our actions—are energies that we release into the world. Those energies return to us multiplied several times over.

The Harris Foundation supports programs in elementary and secondary schools, where we emphasize the importance of discovering abilities early in life. By "discovering," we mean simply paying attention to your abilities, looking for those things that come naturally to you. They may be skills, talents, or just yearnings. They may be strong or silent inner urges to do this or that. But the point is that we are all filled with abilities that are uniquely ours. Some of these we may not share with others, but many are ours to give freely to the world. This is how we grow as individuals.

Our lives are filled with opportunities to know, grow, and share. Many of us are afraid of what we will uncover in our soul searching. We are fearful that we will finally have to follow through with something, to take action and accomplish something. We are paralyzed by the old "fear of success" that has been talked about by so many experts.

The seeds were planted for The Harris Foundation in 1995, when NASA received a routine request from the Harris County Juvenile Probation Department. They wanted an astronaut to speak at a groundbreaking ceremony with a "moon" theme. I wasn't exactly the go-to guy for volunteer work at the agency, but I was one of those who never said no.

At the ceremony, I was struck by the number of kids who were just drifting through the day, existing in a state of hopelessness. Some were in denial; they knew nothing good was in store for them, but they were uncertain what to expect. Most were frightened, but they were trying hard not to show it.

Carole Allen, then the public communication officer for the Harris County Juvenile Probation Department, had guided me to the fifth floor of the Youth Detention Center on West Dallas, in a scruffy part of downtown Houston. The situation was a sobering one to walk into; everybody went through a metal screening detector. The administrators were glad to have me there and pleased that I would talk to the group. But I still had to be checked out and approved to get inside.

I met with a group of fifty boys, all wearing orange jumpsuits, in a room that was sterile and bleak, with walls painted gray. There were no bars in the areas reserved for juveniles, but the room was very secure, with lots of locks on the doors. No one was allowed to leave the floor without an escort.

No one smiled. I was told, and I knew instinctively, that the young people who fall into trouble with the law usually have problems at home. Often they have no real role model there, and almost always they lived under grim economic conditions, in situations where parents struggled to pay the rent and put food on the table. Many of the kids had only one parent at home, and the missing parent was usually the father, the home split by divorce, drugs, booze, or domestic violence—everything a child should ideally not be exposed to.

Most of the kids never knew the possibilities for them out in the world. If they floundered in school, there didn't seem to be any hope anywhere else. If the neighborhood had a church, and their mother could get them to go, or if the church had an outreach program, that might be the only chance they had to see someone who was successful.

When I went to the front of the room to begin my talk, I saw that I was facing an audience that was touchy and bored. I hadn't expected a cheerful visit, but I wasn't prepared for the anguish I felt. The air of depression was like a slap across the face. I knew many of the kids were from Houston's Third or Fifth wards, areas where gang activity flourished and crime was rampant.

I sensed this feeling of despair. I didn't relate to it or fully grasp their individual pain, but I recognized the signs. I had spent my early years in a strained household, but my mother left my father because she didn't want to raise her kids around a drunk. She had an education and would become a teacher. So we had options.

My only goal at that moment was to give the young men some glimmer of hope—a thought, however slim, that they could break out of the cycle of poverty and disorder. After I introduced myself, I began telling my story, relaying the issues early in my life, the escape to a new environment, and the revelation of my dream. I also shared with them what it was like to travel in space. The more I shared my own story with them, the more I felt that I was reaching out to them in a meaningful way. So, I posed a question: "What are you going to do when you leave this place?" They looked back at me with blank stares. "Okay, how about this: Are you going to go back to school?" Again, nothing.

As I stared at their blank faces, I had an "Aha!" moment. I asked my final question: "How many of you know what you what to do when you grow up?" Only two hands were raised. As a "rocket scientist," I had finally figured it out—the boys sitting before me lacked the ability to see themselves in the future. They had lost the ability to dream.

I then began to talk to them about what they wanted to do after they "got past" the situation they were in—what plans they had. One realistic young man said he'd like to be in the military. Most, however, said they wanted to play either professional football or basketball. One short, stocky young man caught my eye, and when I asked him what he wanted to do with his life, he said simply, "Hoops."

I invited him to come up and stand beside me. He didn't reach my shoulder.

I said, "You know, I'm six feet three, and when I was in high school I thought it would be great to play in the NBA or NFL. But somewhere along the way, I realized I wasn't going to be good enough or tall enough. I knew I needed to think about finding another path if I wanted to succeed." I wasn't trying to embarrass anyone. I just wanted to give them a dose of reality—and encouragement.

They really could turn their lives around, I told them, but they had to have as much education as they could get. There was no other way. They knew I was an astronaut and a doctor. With each career path I chose, I pointed out, my life grew better.

I left frustrated because there was little that could be done right then, right there. I began to do my own research to figure out a way to reach those kids. I talked to the director of the Harris County Juvenile Probation Department, to teachers and counselors, to principals and others. I asked each of them,

"How early can you identify these children as problems?" The answer that I got was startling: in elementary school and sometimes even in kindergarten. Wow, what an eye opener!

I realized the best way to approach the problem would be to start with younger kids. I spoke with Carole Allen, and she agreed to help. That was when we started talking about organizing the Dare to Dream program and offering it at the elementary age.

After that visit, I began to make an annual trip to the detention center just before Christmas. I talk to everyone in there—a hundred and fifty kids, girls as well as boys. I make the same point at every visit: They can do anything they want in life, but they absolutely *must* have an education. They have to get back into school and focus on it.

I try to reach out to all of them, but if I suspect there may be one child who needs a little extra attention, I will seek him or her out and take a question or two, privately.

Carole began to work for Dare to Dream out of her office in the Juvenile Probation Department. She rarely misses a chance to pay me a compliment, and I ought to acknowledge that here.

You think of all the years he has done this, yet he continues with the same enthusiasm. The more he gets to do, the more he does. It is amazing to me. I know he feels some sympathy for the ones who never had a break.

I remember the first time I heard the story of how his mother went to work as a cook and waitress in a diner in Waco, and when Bernard and his younger brother would go with her, they had to go in through the back door. I got tears in my eyes; one of the most outstanding people you will ever meet and he had to use the back door.

We can't say for certain what impact we have had on the lives of these detainees. The problem with tracking kids in the juvenile population is that you are limited by confidentiality laws. But Carole hears from some, and our office gets a call or an e-mail now and then from one who finished high school or even college, or found a job. Sometimes the mothers stay in touch.

In the Houston area alone, the program now serves more than three hundred students across ten schools, and the program kicks off each year with my visit to the first school, where I distribute cards with my personal credo, the ABCs, which stands for "I can *Achieve*, if I *Believe* and *Conceive* my dream."

When Carole and I first talked that day in the detention center about what could be done, she jumped on my ABC mantra. "That," she said, "will be the basis the program should build this on—your belief, the convictions that make Bernard Harris tick. That is what this program is going to run on."

I had received a check for $500 a few days earlier from Time Warner Cable after being selected for the Hometown Hero award. We had already signed up a couple of grade schools, so I said, "Let's use that money to buy T-shirts for the kids with the slogan Dare to Dream across the front."

I am proud and a bit stunned that a small, local speaking engagement had such a profound effect on me and so many others. I had already made the decision to leave the space program and head for the business world, but something about these young people grabbed me.

Cosponsored by the Harris County Juvenile Probation Department and Communities in Schools, the Dare to Dream program had an immediate impact. With our cosponsors, we developed a nine-month campaign that boosts self-esteem in elementary and middle school children by providing them access to positive role models. We use an interactive math and science curriculum, as well as career discussions with astronauts and other professionals, to get students thinking about their futures and exploring the possibilities that were out there waiting to be picked, like low-hanging fruit.

Carole Allen's daughter, Jane Stones, wrote the curriculum that covers three elements for the student participants. The first element, "My Self," includes an assortment of tests and drills that stress loyalty and honesty.

The second element, "My Community" emphasizes neighborhood projects such as food drives, cleanups, and school-centered projects. One student launched a project to work on ending the abuse of animals, and he brought in someone from the Humane Society to talk with the students. Others have written cards and letters to kids in the Texas Children's

Hospital and visited nursing homes. The idea is to encourage the kids to think beyond themselves.

The third curriculum element, "My World," focuses on taking kids to local college campuses, such as the University of Houston, Rice University, and Texas Southern University, and other places that represent a new, positive environment for them. When we started the pilot program in 1995 at R. P. Harris Elementary (no relation), we could not have imagined how much the teachers would love it. Obviously, the idea was something that could be replicated at other schools. As teachers moved on to new schools, they wanted to introduce the program there as well, having seen how well it works. We have to restrict the schools to ten in Houston because the program is limited by the number of probation officers who are able to volunteer, but now Dare to Dream is spreading to other counties and school districts.

The program also offers a presentation about careers. We have FBI agents, police officers, and probation officers speak in the schools, and it is amazing (and perhaps ironic) how many kids end up saying they want to be a police officer or a probation officer. The speakers are usually people who can present a smooth, measured talk, and the kids are attracted to that. Juvenile probation officers also have volunteered to visit the schools regularly, reinforcing my message of the ABCs as well as the need for self-esteem, responsibility, and getting along with others.

Throughout the year, the students perform at least two community service projects. They also keep journals, monitored by school officials, which track their progress. In the end, Dare to Dream has resulted in students having an increased desire to stay in school, dream of successful careers, and set their goals for achievement.

By 1998, it was clear that we needed a more formal structure to manage our growing interests, so I founded The Harris Foundation, a nonprofit based in Houston. But we knew that these innovative, classroom-based ideas would work anywhere. Overall, our mission is to empower youth and communities, especially minorities and the economically and/or socially disadvantaged, to develop their full potential and pursue their dreams through national education, health, and wealth programs.

As mentioned earlier, giving doesn't happen in a vacuum, and some of the energies we release into the world return to us multiplied several times over. Some of that energy returned to The Harris Foundation in January 2010. Janice Ford Griffin, a key member of our Harris Foundation team, had moved from Houston to Princeton, New Jersey, to join the staff of the Robert Wood Johnson Foundation, the largest philanthropy devoted exclusively to the health and health care of all Americans. For three years, Janice administered the Community Health Leaders Award program, which elevates the visibility of leaders through a national, $125,000 award and networking opportunities. Today there are 178 community health leader honorees in forty-five states and Puerto Rico.

We were approached about the possibility of establishing a strategic alliance with the Robert Wood Johnson Foundation.

Janice would return to Houston, and the Community Health Leaders Award program would be based at The Harris Foundation.

The fit was ideal. The Robert Wood Johnson Foundation noted that we offered "a new, rich network that can help expand the outreach for nominations of new leaders, as well as reach new venues for increasing the visibility of current ones." I saw this union as a unique chance to support the exceptional men and women working to address the health care problems facing their communities.

By now I hope you have a sense that everything and everyone is connected. So what we do on a given day affects what happens on the next, and also affects those around us. If we are highly successful, then those around us gain as well. Look at Bill Gates, whose dream led him to become the richest person in the world. Even though he is a billionaire, he has created a number of other billionaires and many more millionaires in the process of fulfilling his own dreams.

How astonishing is it to realize that more than forty years have passed since the first moon landing? My mission during my tenure at NASA was to follow orders as a member of the astronaut corps while, at the same time, accomplishing my dream. My new mission now is to ensure that the youth of America have the same opportunity to follow their dreams.

The Harris Foundation is a large part of that commitment. The Dare to Dream program and the new partnership with the Robert Wood Johnson Foundation provide many opportunities. But education is still the central focus for our outreach efforts with math and science at the forefront.

Chapter 9

Becoming the Science (and Math) Guy

The future depends on what we do in the present.
—Mahatma Gandhi

Dreams are the reality of the future.
—Dr. Bernard A. Harris Jr.

As often happens with ideas large and enduring, this one started off small, with a phone call from the University of Houston.

It was 1995, three years before we officially established The Harris Foundation. The university had received a grant from the National Science Foundation to host a series of camps for high school students. Since I graduated with a degree in biology from the University of Houston and had been honored as a distinguished alumnus they asked me if they could name the program in my honor. The science camps fit with my personal strategy of utilizing education for achievement, so naturally I said yes.

Over the next couple of years the camps made a significant impact on the students' lives and were very effective in capturing students' interest in math and science. These subjects were meaningful to the students. The Houston Independent School

District was already involved, and UH caught a break because the district's manager of science was a wonderful lady named Barbara Foots.

After the University of Houston funding from the National Science Foundation was over, I agreed to take it on personally. I tapped into the only other government agency I knew: NASA. Once I submitted a proposal to Johnson Space Center, the program was funded and we were off and running. Naturally, I asked Barbara Foots to work with me. We met and designed the first camp, which initially had twenty-one students.

Our first year we recruited a faculty who not only could teach but also had good ideas on the direction of the camps to help us flesh out some of our own. The program was based on Barbara's experience as an educator and science coordinator for twenty years, and on my desire to reach the youth of America. Since the inception of the Bernard Harris Summer Science Camp, we have reached out to thousands of kids in communities across this country.

I remember one kid in particular because he was not chosen by the camp. This boy's mother told one of the counselors she needed desperately to get her son in the program. He was sixteen and on the verge of dropping out of school. His parents had divorced, and he was unhappy because the father had moved out of town and he had no contact with him. The young man had just given up. We ended up with one slot open in his grade level. We were trying to ensure ethnic diversity, and he was an exact match.

The camp inspired him. He finished high school and went off to college. I felt really good that we were able to salvage the education of a child who had made up his mind to drop out. He went on to graduate from Texas Southern University.

In a nutshell, this was what we had envisioned as the mandate for the camps: to motivate the students, instill a sense of purpose in them, and encourage them to complete their education.

We were able to attract splendid instructors, who were the key to the program. One was Jennifer Williams, who helped find others who majored in psychology or child development, and we put together a good team. Two other teachers, Carmelita Landry and Cheryl Willis, took the lead in monitoring how the kids behaved in the cafeteria, what kind of activities they responded to, and how they acted in a group setting. Our teachers helped shape the training system.

Robbie Evans, with the Urban Experience program at the University of Houston, recommended college students as counselors. They were closer to the ages of the campers and helped create a different environment. They were able to help with discipline and to tell us what the kids wanted in the way of recreation. They had a keen eye for what worked and helped us revise and update the program.

Shortening the camp to two weeks; targeting students in grades six, seven, and eight; and focusing on science, technology, engineering, and mathematics (STEM) were key elements of the program. We also adopted a policy to enroll equal numbers of girls and boys. There was some concern about accepting kids coming out of the sixth grade and going into a residential program. But Barbara Foots had a soft spot for the younger ones. "Don't worry about my babies," she told the skeptics. "They will get help from the eighth-graders, and vice versa." And it worked out exactly that way.

We knew we had to identify the students early if we were to make a definite impact. By the time they were in high school, it was too late to change some of the choices they had made. We developed our criteria: First, the kids must perform academically to show they have the ability to achieve; they need to have at least a B average. Second, the students have to be recommended by two teachers. Third, the students have to write an essay on why they want to attend the camp and on their interest in math and science.

In 1997, we added a second campus after receiving a request from Southwestern Oklahoma State University. The student population included a number of Native Americans, which was important to me, given my experiences living in the Navajo Nation. An effort would be made to seek out kids who were traditionally overlooked. Our core curriculum would continue to be based on the relatively new STEM initiatives appearing across the country.

Most of our academic needs had been met, and I wanted to expand the concept and take it to other cities and states. But an immediate problem confronted us, and it could not be ignored or postponed: funding. I wanted our program to have a greater impact on the educational issues facing America, and we could not afford to go it alone. Even with NASA's support through the years, from Johnson Space Center and later NASA Headquarters, it was a huge undertaking.

Meanwhile, my friend and fraternity brother at the University of Houston had become the president of the ExxonMobil Foundation in Dallas. When Gerald McElvy and I were in school, we sometimes joked about how one day we would be rich and famous, in a position to make a difference. Now I made an appointment to meet with Gerald and Truman Bell, the company's senior program officer. Truman and I had met when I spoke in Phoenix to a minority engineering organization whose board he was on. He recalled that I talked about my dream, about how kids should dream and have goals in life.

Our track record was fine, given that we had worked with both the National Science Foundation and NASA for a number of years. Truman admitted that the foundation was not really looking for a new project. But our timing was fortunate. Gerald and Truman were working on an updated education strategy for ExxonMobil, expanding upon their already strong investment in education. A big part of that, math and science and technology, had been a central element because it spoke to the nature of their company.

One of the things they had learned a long time ago was that some programs are difficult to work with and problematic. Their niche, therefore, was in the professional development of teachers.

They figured if they could invest in teachers, they would reach tens of thousands of kids. Our science camp directly targets the student, and this was a new approach for the foundation.

They had begun to refocus because of a couple of things. The most important was a study done by the National Academy of Sciences, called "Rising Above the Gathering Storm," published in 2005. This study was alarming because it concluded that if the United States system didn't take action today to improve in math and science education, we would lose our competitive edge in the future. The United States used to be one of the highest-ranked countries in the world in terms of math and science education, but we had slipped to twenty-eighth among the top thirty-five industrial nations. This hit close to home, because when Truman made speeches at a university, he would say, "If you love math and science, you will love ExxonMobil because that's what we do twenty-four hours a day."

Truman and I had a Texas Tech connection, as well. He worked on the staff at Tech as director of career services in the late 1970s. So we were able to talk Red Raider stuff together, and it all sort of clicked. I left their offices allowing myself to feel somewhat optimistic. You do not always like or feel impressed with people whom you ask for money and who have the power to say no. But I knew McElvy and instinctively trusted Bell. I felt as though the two of them cared about education and understood what we were trying to accomplish.

We scheduled the next meeting at our offices in Houston. I laid out what the funding would look like and what it would take to get the camps restarted. Gerald and Truman listened to my pitch; it must have sounded pretty good, because they agreed to fund me. They agreed that their company would do its part.

I was surprised and impressed when they came back and said that they wanted to provide funding and that they wanted to include NASA. In 2005, NASA had cut most of the funding for its education programs, including my summer science camps in Houston and Oklahoma. The space agency was hurting from budget cuts, but the ExxonMobil Foundation offered to come up with part of the money. So, we did two pilot camps that summer with support from ExxonMobil and NASA, at the University of Houston and Southwest Oklahoma State University. It was a tremendous success!

NASA dropped out after the next summer, and I learned later that Truman and Gerald were prepared to pick up the slack. I found out later that Truman said, "This is too good a program to risk losing it. But we're not making a big impact with two camps. We should take this nationwide. You can do this at any university. Bernard has the staff. They know how to do it."

They could have done the math and decided the price was too high in terms of cost, but we knew that the results and rewards would be priceless. The ExxonMobil Foundation tied this into a big announcement in October. They had a big press conference, with the CEO and chairman of the board, Rex Tillerson, to announce this major funding in the STEM area. The foundation also had a partnership with Phil Mickelson, one of the world's top golfers, and his foundation to do professional development training for teachers—the Mickelson ExxonMobil Teachers Academy. Phil came to the press conference, as did the president of the University of Texas, because they were going to take the university's innovative UTeach program nationally. I was there too. We each spoke.

ExxonMobil understood the issue highlighted by "Rising Above the Gathering Storm," and they were going to do something about it and greatly increase what they were doing. Things are really rigorous with a program like this. They write up the evaluations, go through the modifications with management, and get them approved. At around five o'clock that afternoon, everything was completed and the press release was ready to go. And I said, "I'm really excited about all this. I've talked to my foundation staff, and we believe that we can do the ten camps."

Truman and Gerald said, "What do you mean, *ten* camps? We're planning on doing *twenty* camps!"

I replied, "My understanding was that we were starting with ten. Twenty may be a real stretch."

Truman said, "Look, I've written a speech for the chairman of the board saying we're doing twenty camps. I'm not going back to him and saying we're doing only ten."

So I said, "Okay, it's going to be hard, but we can get it done." Twenty camps was a big jump and meant a thousand students would go through the program. The following year we went to twenty-five camps and then to thirty, and that reached about fifteen hundred students across the nation.

—

I try not to overanalyze the success of the camps. But they work! The universities, the teachers, the students—they all make different but essential contributions to the program. They come up with ideas that don't repeat the classes they had during the regular school year. We let the students experiment. They build rockets and rafts. They take field trips to places they have never been. For example, if they had to identify certain plants in school, we take them to an arboretum.

Another innovation was graduation day, a program that the students design and organize. They receive certificates or plaques, but the good work is their real reward. Whatever the outcome of their learning, it has to be in the form of a project or a presentation.

When we expanded from one to two and then to four, and then to twenty camps, we came out with something called media day. This was a chance for the host university to invite the local media to see whatever was going on. I attend as many of these events as I can make and speak to the students. We wanted to have one activity for every camp that could serve as an example of science-as-education-plus-fun. This is an opportunity for us to spread the word throughout the community about the program and the need for STEM education.

Our standards are strict; our bar is set high. We hire people who create experiments that challenge the kids. Then, both the staff and the students evaluate the program. The students are always totally honest about what they like and what they don't.

The Raft Rally, an experiment with an aluminum raft, turned

out to be very popular. The kids are divided into teams, with each receiving four straws and two sheets of aluminum foil. The competition is to construct a raft in ten or fifteen minutes and then see which raft has the most buoyancy. We tested them in a tub of water, dropping in pennies to see which one would hold the most before it sank. I think the national record is close to 500 pennies. Designing and building the raft is a true learning experience; the students learn about density, gravity, and all manner of things.

We adjust the training to fit what they enjoy and what provides a benefit. There is very little turnover among the teachers. They want to come back, and the only time we lose any is when they change jobs or move out of town.

Our expectations are high. We may send a student home if he or she violates the rules, and once in a while one will leave because of homesickness. These are middle school kids, after all. But if they stay for any length of time, they will learn something and they will be changed. That is why we spend the time to select the right kids. You start out with forty-eight and end up with forty-eight, and that is not an accident.

Research shows us that if these kids have good grades going into middle school, but maybe they don't have the support system in life, their chances of making it into college majoring in math or science are slim. Many drop out. This in part explains the high dropout rate in this country. But being inspired and having good role models, and finding out what you can really do with math and science, makes a big difference.

We have guidelines, structure, and accountability. The kids are involved, they are engaged, and an overwhelming good number go on to college, where many major in fields such as engineering, biology, and sciences.

In 2008, again with a grant from ExxonMobil, The Harris Foundation launched another traveling road show called the DREAM Tour. DREAM stands for "Daring to Reach Excellence for America's Minds." This motivational program encourages America's middle school students to both discover and achieve their potential. It explains that they can do this by going to college and pursuing careers in science, technology, engineering, and math, the four STEM disciplines.

In a nice rounding of the circle, we kicked off the first DREAM Tour, our inaugural journey, with a visit to the school that two years earlier had been named in my honor in San Antonio, the Bernard Harris Middle School. How cool is that? In keeping with the boundless ambitions of the science camps and the Dare to Dream program, which strives to prevent juvenile delinquency, the goals for the DREAM Tour are lofty. We want to make rock stars of our highest achievers, and this recognition program is called the Rock Stars of STEM.

During the interactive program for the students, we bring out two of the chairs used on an actual space shuttle and have one boy and one girl sit in them. I describe the sensations of liftoff and tell the group about walking in space. It is an exciting program for the students.

One of the aspects of the program that is most impactful is our emphasis on the personal growth of the individual student. In one part of the program, we ask them to repeat this statement: "I am an infinite being with infinite possibilities."

After they repeat this phrase after me three times, I then tell them why.

Knowing who you really are is important in life. The earlier this discovery about yourself happens, the more likely you are to achieve. So, spend time thinking about that. There are three things that I believe about you:

1. You are multi-talented.
2. You have multi-potential.
3. You were born for a reason.

First, I believe that you were born with talents and abilities that are uniquely yours. No one else can do the things that you do in your own way. If you think about it long enough, you will realize what I say is true. We all have abilities—some we know about and some are yet to be discovered. So, your first job is figure what those talents are . . . and only you can do this. Second, you have the ability to do anything you want. A simple statement but true. This means that you have unlimited potential—inborn energy that gives you the power to carry out any accomplishment that you desire. Finally, I believe that you were born for a reason. Your birth was no accident! You are here for a reason . . . you are here to do something special. You are special! The earlier you realize this, the better.

So, the phrase "I am an infinite being with infinite possibilities" is my way of relaying to the kids the power that they have inside. They must begin to think about their future now, prepare for that future now . . . because their dreams are the reality of the future.

The ultimate objective for the DREAM Tour is to reach one million students, teachers, and parents before the end of the year 2010. We visited eleven schools in 2008 and fifteen schools in 2009. Thus far we have been to Chicago, Detroit, New York, Los Angeles, Miami, Dallas, and many more cities. To date the DREAM Tour has resulted in more than fifty million impressions, meaning the message about STEM education is getting out in a big way, far exceeding our goal of one million!

In December 2009, we brought the DREAM Tour to the Toyota Center, the luxurious arena where the Houston Rockets play their NBA home games. Students from the Houston Independent School District and three other school systems showed up as part of a crowd numbering approximately ten thousand, an organizational feat of considerable distinction. The students arrived in one hundred school buses and viewed a two-hour program that included one of my motivational speeches; a dance number by some of our middle school Dreamers; and antics by Clutch, the Rockets' mascot. We also showed a number of commercials that I was in: Microsoft's "I'm a PC" ad campaign,

Cadillac, H-E-B, and of course, ExxonMobil's television campaign. The kids really got excited by my cameo appearance in the "Men in Black II" music video, from the movie that featured Will Smith and Tommy Lee Jones. I'm not sure what I was doing in the video, but there I was.

The sport mascots had flash cards that read on one "Science" and on another "Math," and they held them up on cue and the kids screamed. I am not sure that the Rockets have heard that much noise, at least not since their championship seasons in the mid-1990s. The whole show was geared for these kids aged eleven to fourteen, and it was a sight to behold—a *pep rally* for math and science!

What needs to be kept in mind is the fact that these subjects need promoting and need selling because they are hard. Even the kids who are gifted need to be reminded that they are worthy and need to be nurtured. This program and all our education programs embody these principles and are geared to reach the students where they are, not force them to come to us. This is a very important aspect to remember, if we are to truly effect change and motivate our youth.

I was asked to give a lecture at Northeastern University in Boston in 2008, to discuss STEM education with a group of leaders. These included representatives and staff for several of the colleges and universities in Boston, such as Harvard, Boston University, MIT, and Northeastern as well as community and program leaders and parents. Following my talk, we had a dialogue about the issues and needs for STEM education. It was eye-opening for me. I discovered that there are many other people concerned about the state of education in this country, and that a number of efforts are being made not only in Boston but also around the nation to address these issues and provide solutions. More important, I learned that I was not alone.

I returned to Houston with a new mission: to find a way to engage leaders in each of the communities that we are touring. I wanted to create a program where educators, parents, government officials, and concerned citizens could come together to learn and to exchange knowledge and experience about education in this country. So, we created the Educational Forum: Listening to America. Now at every stop we make on the DREAM Tour, we hold this forum the night before the program for the kids. It has been extremely successful! This program has resulted in the sharing and networking opportunities that have generated many pearls of wisdom about education. This knowledge and experience is being recorded for publication and is soon to be shared with the rest of the nation.

This is my new mission: to save as many kids as I can. Achieving a certain level of fame as an astronaut has given me the platform to do this for American youth. This is why I have flown up to twenty-five of the thirty ExxonMobil Bernard Harris Summer Science Camp locations each year. I think of it as my summer vacation. I am flattered when people, especially those in ventures with me, wonder how I am able to travel 225 days a year to support these programs. Truman Bell jokingly calls me the Energizer Bunny. I don't really have an answer. It's true, I actually have a day job with my venture capital company, Vesalius Ventures, and I still work as a physician.

These programs are important to me . . . and to the nation. So, I do as much as I can.

Chapter 10

THE POWER WITHIN

*One person with a belief is equal to a force
of ninety-nine who have only interests.*
—John Stuart Mill

When I was an undergraduate at the University of Houston, I attended a lecture where we discussed the importance of God in the lives of great individuals. The search for God has been the catalyst for the growth of some of the most significant figures in human history. From Lincoln agonizing over the dogs of war to Martin Luther King confronting the dogs of Birmingham—philosophers, inventors, and martyrs alike have sought divine guidance.

I have always believed in God. Although I am not religious in an organized way, I am a spiritual person. It is less meaningful to me to worship with many, than to have a personal relationship with God and what I call the Universal Presence.

Many have asked me how my travels in space changed my perspective. Traveling in space has simply confirmed my belief. You cannot venture into space, see the vastness of the universe, look down and see the world below, and not be convinced that there is something more than your senses can perceive.

Seeing the Earth from space gave me a different perspective, similar to the one that I believe God would approve—that we are one people without differences. From space you cannot see differences between countries. You cannot see the different races and ethnic groups. From space there is simply one Earth with one people.

It is only when you come closer that you see the division of the people in the world; when you notice that people are treated differently based on their ethnic background, their wealth, and their social status. This division is not reserved for the developed countries, but occurs in the developing countries, too. Racism and prejudice have no favorites. Unfortunately, many with wealth and power may not see it, and therefore they see no need to change the status quo, which affects their own livelihoods.

The astronaut's perspective allows one to see things a little differently. As Martin Luther King, Jr., proclaimed, "I have been to the mountaintop." In this case, the mountaintop is space itself. For first-timers, it is like being in a dream when you look out the window of the spaceship to observe the Earth below, and you are awestruck by the sheer beauty of what you see. There is the Earth from which you came, in all its majesty, suspended in time and space, a mostly blue planet with swirls of clouds on a backdrop of an endless sea of stars. It is beyond anything that one can imagine while standing here on Earth. Although we have captured this image in TV, in pictures, and on film, these images cannot do justice to the live experience.

—

Seeking a new perspective, whether by walking in space or simply taking a step back from the situation here on Earth, can make a crucial difference in a person's attitude. When I speak to youth groups, I always emphasize to them that their attitude determines their altitude: how and what you think affects how high you will rise. If your mind is always thinking about the worst that can happen, then the worst usually happens. You will be caught up in a negative cycle, and your growth as an individual will stagnate. Your mind will focus only on the negative aspects of your life.

But if you turn toward the light, to the brighter aspects, to those things that uplift you, then your future will be entirely different. Your perspective will change, allowing you to receive the good life. Your attitude will change, and you will rise up out of the depths of futility and reach a new realm of possibility. So, indeed, your attitude determines your altitude. This principle applies not only to the youth of this world, but to everyone who wants fulfillment in their lives.

We citizens of Earth spend an exorbitant amount of time separating ourselves into special groups. We are territorial, dividing the world in which we live, determining how places and people should be separated. I believe this is an attempt to gain some element of acceptance in a world of divided loyalties and alliances. As part of a small, culturally diverse community, I learned at a very young age to deal with many different types of people.

This skill is essential, and it is one I still use every day. I believe that we are all born with unlimited potential, with the ability to do all things. I believe that when we enter this world, there are no limits in our minds. In fact it is just the opposite. It is only after we experience our first failure that we begin to think differently. We let poverty, divorce, hate, disappointment, and fear limit us. How do I know this? Because I have experienced and suffered through each of these. I am no different from most of us in this respect.

Find your calling, your talent, your special purpose, and you will find a vision for your life. Sometimes it comes as trial and error. But defeat is never more certain than when you resign yourself to it. People who are perpetually lost will do desperate things to find themselves.

Many of us walk around all day in dread, expecting bad things to happen. Others are so afraid of making mistakes or being wrong, they avoid the risk of being successful. Still others let fear drive them into solitude, nonaction, or withdrawal. We must all learn to overcome fear. How? By meeting it head-on: First, by recognizing that it is there. Second, by acknowledging the impact that it has on us. Finally, by willing ourselves to be brave enough to face our doubts. Use your fears to grow.

It is scary to be out front, and people who are there put their lives on the line. These are also the people who do great things in life. We look up to them and then ask, why are they so lucky?

Eddie Rickenbacker, a World War I hero and pioneer aviator, once said, "I believe that if you think about disaster, you will get it. Brood about death, and you hasten your demise. Think positively and masterfully, with confidence and faith, and life becomes more secure, more fraught with action, richer in achievement and experience."

When Armstrong and Aldrin stepped onto the face of the moon, this one event inspired a national pride that America had not experienced since World War II. If humans could land on the moon, we could accomplish anything; this is how the whole country felt at the time. This was not only a giant leap for mankind but a milestone for a new generation. As I discovered my dream to be an astronaut, the moment defined me. I learned who I really was: an unlimited being with the power to do anything I set my mind to.

How do you discover this? If you are lost, how do you figure out what there is for you to do in this world? You must first decide that you want a different life and that you want a change toward success. Then, you must summon up the courage to take action.

Success is a choice that you make. Success does not come by accident. A gauge of success is not whether you have a tough problem to solve, but whether it is the same problem you had last month or last year. Failure can be divided into two types: those who thought and never did, and those who did and never thought.

—

Achievement, on the other hand, can be divided into an infinite number of groups according to many different strengths—and many hardships that have been overcome. Many Americans have ancestors who were taken away from their homelands and brought here by force, to a place where their only value was providing free labor for the architects of this country. In other words, America was built on the backs of its underclass. When I mention this, you might think that I am referring to African-Americans. In fact, African-Americans were not the only ones victimized by a system of forced or cheap labor.

Asian Americans were also used as cheap labor, and so were several groups of European descent, including the Irish and the Italians, and let's not forget the Hispanic Americans in the past and even now. The Native Americans also took a tremendous loss in land and in life. I do not want to trivialize any one group's contribution, but only to point out that many different groups are indeed responsible for building this country as we know it today.

Yet there are still cynics who think differently. The following is a letter that I received after my first walk in space. The author shall remain anonymous. His letter begins:

> I note by newspaper reports that you, as the first Afro-astro to take a spacewalk, are taking with you the flag of the Navajo Nation to plant in space.
>
> How "wonderful." What historic minority exhibitionism and, I should add, what minority racism all of this indicates. An Afro astronaut has to take his first

spacewalk and use it as a minority pitch. The people at the space program who have permitted you to get by with this nonsense should hide their heads in shame.

When I think how the U.S. program had its foundations established by the genius of the German scientists many years ago, and that it has now in recent years become a launching ground in the recruitment and encouragement of minority students and engineers, I become outraged. And now this nonsense on top of it all.

And he goes on to say:

Ironically, this symbolizes how minority races have climbed to the stars on the shoulders of the white race and its scientific genius, out of a stupid generosity and unnecessary guilt complex in relation to racial minorities.

Of course, everyone is entitled to an opinion, and that is among the things that make America great: You can voice your opinion without being targeted. It is certainly easier for the people in power to make their opinions known without reprisal, but the same is not true for many in this country. As Oliver Wendell Holmes stated, "The mind of the bigot is like the pupil of the eye; the more light you pour upon it, the more it will contract."

—

In the face of arguments from closed and angry minds that see no value in diversity and no unity among mankind, one of the most important tools for success is empowerment. What do I mean by "empowerment"? Endowing a person, or a people, with the power to overcome adversity, whatever it is and whatever the source. Empowerment is something that many lack—even the person who wrote the "outraged" letter to me. If we have true power, power that comes from within, we can stand firm against the forces who wish us ill. My sister has a quote that she uses as a tag on her e-mail: "Adversity helps us to know who we are!" She learned this, as we all have, the hard way: by living and learning through the adversity of our family lives. She used this as a stepping stone to achieve her own successes. I have learned a great deal by watching her.

How do you empower yourself? First, by recognizing where your strength comes from, figuring out who you are, and what you want out of life. Second, by identifying your weakness, your Achilles' heel or your kryptonite. Once you know this, you can begin to work on eliminating or overcoming it. For some, this might include getting more education. For others, it might be improving the ability to tolerate emotional stress.

One of the first things my mother taught me was to believe in God. I come from a traditional African-American family, so there was no question of whether He existed. God was at the heart of my family as far back as I can remember. My great-grandmother was the matriarch of the family. Her exploits in

His name were stories of legend. She was noted for praying and healing. Her belief in a Heavenly Father led her to become a successful leader in the community. We were taught to pray as though everything depended on God, but work as though everything depended on us.

I believe the ultimate "high" is fulfilling your dreams. To be able to honestly say that I set a goal and accomplished it is a high greater than you can imagine. I have had several highs in life, as physician, astronaut, and venture capitalist. Still, too many of us have discovered that success is as fleeting as smoke or as a butterfly that eludes us at every turn.

When was the last time you attended a musical concert, where a band or orchestra was playing and you truly listened? If you really paid attention, you probably noticed that the band was made up of individual members, each of whom is talented in his or her individual instrument. Alone, the individual parts may not make sense, but together they make beautiful music that touches the hearts of those listening.

Likewise in life we are all caught up in the moment and the music, feeling that we are a part of a universe that encompasses all that is good in life. We are on top of the world, nothing is wrong, and everything is in order. What a great feeling, a tremendous view, or an endless joy.

If we play our own instrument the very best we can, then we become part of a symphony much greater than ourselves, and we live our lives in harmony with the universe. This is why it is so important to reach your full potential. We are all connected, no matter how small or big we think we are. Just pay attention to your environment and you'll see this truth.

God is omnipresent. If you think about it, the only thing that great scientists really do is describe the world that already exists. We humans do not create anything that has not already been created.

I anguished about including a chapter in the book that talked about the power within and the power of God. But this is who I am. A book about me and my achievements would not capture the full essence of who I am without this discussion. It's not only that I want you to know me; I also hope you use the pages in this book to enable the power from within you, too.

As I reflect, I am struck by the demonstration of this power in my life. It began with the escape from poverty and my mother's decision to get a divorce. This was a very painful time for me and the whole family, but it was a necessary event that led us to the promised land of the Navajo Nation. I cannot understate the impact of these people on me and my life. Their spiritual nature combined with mine to enrich me in ways I still have yet to discover.

Here are some points that may assist you in finding the power within:

- Belief starts with you! You must believe in yourself and in those who believe in you. The first step in setting out to accomplish anything begins with a whole-hearted belief in your abilities. Without that fundamental faith, it is difficult to do anything in life. Without that belief the lens through which you see the world makes everything around you seem dull and uninteresting. If you do not have this confidence, you will lack the initiative that it takes to accomplish your goals and realize your dreams. Life will have no meaning for you. In fact, if you do not believe in yourself no one else will.

- Take the time to examine your belief system and its origins. Ask yourself these questions: What do I believe? Whom do I believe? Whom do I believe in? Belief in God requires that you believe in something or someone greater that yourself.

- Find the thing that makes you happy. Surround yourself with those people who lift you up and do not bring you down.

Many have talked about how to tap into the source of unlimited personal power. If you find your inner power, then you will discover your full potential and empower your life. Internal strength is the key to unlimited power. Internal strength is derived from knowing your true abilities.

Try this exercise:

1. Find a quiet place to be alone, where you will not be disturbed. Relax and clear your mind of all the activities of the day. As you do this, begin to think about your childhood. Go back to when you had no limitations,

when you simply asked and you received. You said, "I want some candy," and candy appeared like magic. At least, that may have been the way it happened for some people. But you get the picture. This was a time when there were no obstacles, when the word "no" had no meaning, a time when your imagination was unlimited. You saw something done and automatically thought that it was possible.

2. While you're back in that time, think about a dream that you had when you were a child. Some of you may have to think harder than others. When you think about the dream, how does it make you feel? Happy? Excited? Are you still yearning to do it? Now think about this: If you were given the opportunity to redo your life and vocation, would you choose the same goals? Or would you do it differently? Would you take a chance?

3. Now that you have conjured up those old desires and ambitions, ask yourself this question: Is it too late to do it? Is it too late to become it? What is your answer? I will tell you the answer: It is NO! It is never too late to realize your dreams.

4. Create a list of those things that you wanted to do, but didn't. Some people call this the "bucket list." This is the list of things that you desire to do before you "kick the bucket"—that is, before you die. I have always said that when I reach the end of my life, I do not want any regrets. I want at least to have tried to accomplish

the goals that I set for myself. You should do the same thing, too.

Do not let life pass you by without first giving it your best try. And then at least you can say you did your best. There are always tasks that you attempt in life and then fail to accomplish for whatever reason. But if you give it your best and still fail, it is okay. Your conscience and soul will be clear. You simply move on to the next thing that you should do. What I have found is that a failure often leads you down the path toward an even greater goal. And for reasons beyond my understanding, it has always seemed that these events were meant to be.

Take this list now, and combine it with your abilities—the skills that are unique to your being, those things that you do especially well or those qualities for which you are best known. If you don't readily see them, ask your friends to tell you what they are. They may be invisible to us, but others see them. So ask. If you are young, some of these talents may not be fully developed. For those of us who are older, we will have a pretty good idea of our talents or lack thereof. Use these as a starting point for self-discovery.

Understanding these talents, in combination with your goals, will reveal your true destiny as a child of God or, as I also like to say, a child of the universe. As Ralph Waldo Emerson wrote, "Once you make a decision, the universe conspires to make it happen."

I truly believe this; it has worked at every step of my life and career: my acceptance into medical school at Texas Tech, my selection for residency at the Mayo Clinic, my fellowship with the National Research Council at NASA's Ames Research Center, and my selection as a U.S. astronaut. The universe, and in my view, God were involved in every aspect of success in my life.

The next time you go outside, take a minute to notice the wonders around you. The grass, flowers, and trees (natural things); the machinery, cars, and buildings (man-made things); the clouds, sun, and stars (our galaxy). Realize that all of this is the universe and you are a vital part it. In my vernacular, the universe is God.

Bernard shows Senator/Astronaut John Glenn around the SpaceHab facility prior to his first shuttle mission

Gerald McElvy, Bernard, and Truman Bell

Jack Gill presenting Bernard with the 2000 Horatio Alger Award

Sandra and Bernard during his induction into
the Horatio Alger Association

Photo taken with Will Smith during the shooting of the movie Men in Black II

Bernard standing in front of the middle school named in his honor in San Antonio's North East Independent School District

Bernard near his quote on the wall of the middle school

Bernard with Congresswoman Sheila Jackson Lee

Students lining up outside of the Toyota Center in Houston, TX, for the DREAM Tour

Inside the DREAM Tour event

Bernard speaks to ten thousand students during the tour

Bernard at the Houston DREAM Tour

Participants at the Educational Forum

Meeting President Bush

Chapter 11

Epilogue: The View from Space

*You see things; and you say "why?" But I dream things
that never were; and I say "why not?"*
—George Bernard Shaw

As I passed through the Houston airport one day, years ago, a young security guard looked up from rummaging through my baggage and said, "Can I ask you something? When did you first know what you wanted to do in life?"

He must have spotted some of my astronaut insignia. "I guess by the time I was about thirteen years old," I said. "How about you? Is this what you really want to do?"

"No!" he replied, with a grimace. "I'm *lost!*" Then he walked away.

I haven't forgotten that young man. In fact, I see him more and more these days, everywhere I look. So many of us go through life as lost as he was: lost souls, not knowing who we are or where we are going. These feelings transcend all geographic, ethnic, racial, and gender boundaries. It seems they permeate all peoples and cultures.

From an early age I have wondered why things are the way

they are, where we come from, whether we were created or, as so many scientists believe, simply evolved. "Believe" . . . it is a word with such significance in my life. I firmly believe that all the things that we will ever be already exist within us. All the skills, talents, and intelligence are here, in us, at this very moment. We simply need to look for them—or in some cases, rediscover them. Sometimes this requires work on our part, work to figure out who we are and what we want in life. We must spend time with ourselves and, when needed, draw support from others— friends, family, those who care about us.

You may not have been as fortunate as I was to have found your life's dream at an early age. Maybe you have yet to find it. But you never will if you do not take the steps of self-discovery, and those steps begin with your dreams. Dreams are the reality of the future. Without dreams, there is no future. Think about that for a moment. In order to have a great life, you have to set goals for yourself and go after them. If you do not, or you will not, then life will just happen to you, and one day you may find yourself lost, unhappy, without hope, and not knowing who you are, why you are here, or what you can do about it.

A personal insight is worth repeating: To find success, you must dream of a better life. Every year I set aside time to visit the Harris County Juvenile Probation Department, where I talk to young people who have been incarcerated. Many are from disadvantaged backgrounds. As I speak with them, it becomes obvious that they share one trait: the inability to see themselves in the future. No one has ever told them that it is not only okay to dream of a better life, it is necessary. Individuals who cannot see themselves in the future are living just for today. In other words, they are focused on only those things that will take care of their needs for today. And without a vision for the future, and therefore a vision of the consequences of their actions, it is very easy for them to do only whatever is necessary to meet their present needs, including taking from or hurting others who may be in their path. From my experience working with these youth, it is easy to see how they end up in detention. Yet they certainly weren't born this way. It is extremely important that we do whatever is in our power to restore their ability to dream.

I once read an op-ed piece that included a quote by William Raspberry: "You cannot accomplish anything in life that is beyond your ability to imagine." He's talking about vision— visualizing or dreaming of a reality that does not yet exist and then creating that reality. The lesson for us all is to dare to dream about our future, whether that means tomorrow or years from now. Set goals for yourself, no matter your age, and visualize yourself achieving them. Then get busy and make those dreams a reality. It works, and it's one way to build a better life.

I recognize the importance of knowing what you want in life. For many people, it is the most difficult task they will face. In fact, let me modify that statement: It is both the most difficult and the most critical question we must answer. If we do not figure this out, our course through life will be haphazard and incomplete. We must all discover our purpose in life. Spend time with yourself to find your true calling. Only you can do it. No one can do it for you. But once you have discovered it, the realities of the heart can lead to the decisions of the head.

—

My childhood transition from the Navajo Nation to San Antonio provided the backdrop for the discovery of my internal power. My journey thus far had been somewhat challenging, given all the changes that had occurred so early in my life. My saving grace was that I was not alone. I had my family, particularly my mother, to show me the way and sometimes even carry me when I needed it. There were fears along the way that I can't even begin to describe—those things that haunt each of us as we are growing up. The questions of my place in the world and where I would end up were among my biggest challenges at the time, challenges that were compounded by the realities of the middle and high school years. You know what I'm talking about. We all go through it, and most of us overcome it despite ourselves. But some never make it through.

I had forgotten how difficult those years were until I had an opportunity to relive them through my daughter as she has navigated her way through high school. So many emotions, so many issues with family and friends. Most of these problems stem from our need to fit into the world. When you boil it all down, fear is at the heart of the matter. We are all afraid to be left out, afraid that we will not fit in, afraid that we will not become the person that we want to be, or in many cases, afraid that we will not achieve what others expect of us.

The key to overcoming these issues is to discover your internal power. This internal power is far greater than the external power of those things you fear. This power lies in your ability to tap into the unlimited source of self. In doing so, you become unlimited in mind.

Did I understand all this when I was growing up? No. But a part of me understood the power of it all, even though I may not have understood the exact mechanism.

After I realized my capabilities, I found that alone, I could not fulfill my dream. I needed guidance to stay the course. This help I found in mentors, role models—call them what you will. Sometimes I call them "angels," sent to provide guidance during the critical times of life. My early angel was my mother, followed by other members of my family and my friends. Dr. Bryant was a strong source of inspiration for me, even though he may not have realized how important he was.

As I think back on different aspects of my life, I recognize how important I have been in a number of people's lives by just being there, saying the right thing at the right moment, or providing a guiding influence during a critical time. We all serve in this capacity at various times, and others have done the same for us. When we recognize this, our relationships with people take on a new meaning. We become important . . . as we should. Said another way, we are all very important, valuable, and significant to the world. Recognizing this fact should elevate our perception of our true purpose.

—

When I left high school in San Antonio, I had a plan. In my mind I had it all laid out. I would go to college and medical school, complete my residency and fellowship, and then apply to become an astronaut. In my mind, it was a logical progression from point A to point B. Well, I didn't count on being rejected. How could they say no to me after all that I had accomplished? I continued my day-to-day work and eagerly awaited news from NASA. But when I received the telephone call, it wasn't what I had hoped for. After all the dreams and the years of study and sacrifice, NASA said no. But, they saw enough potential to offer me a job at the Johnson Space Center.

Failure is one of the most difficult things we deal with in life. During those times, we feel as though the whole world is against us. We become consumed with our weaknesses and everything that we have done wrong in life. The ironic thing about this mind-set is that it tends to destroy our confidence, setting the stage for more failures.

With time we learn that we are shaped by not only our successes but also our failures. We lose a job, only to find another. We leave a relationship and move on, more aware, sadly, that few things in life last forever. The trick is to discover this truth early enough to prevent the "misery of failure." We are defined by the good and the bad, the accomplishments and the defeats. If we are careful to learn from both, we can attain balance.

As a result of my initial rejection from NASA, what some might call "failure," I not only became a clinical scientist and researcher, I also obtained experience in developing medical technology. In addition, I became a flight surgeon. And, of course, eventually I became an astronaut. Many times I have failed only to be presented with new opportunities to take major steps forward—toward a dream that was not lost.

The job of flying in space is not easy. It stresses you both physically and mentally. I managed to survive the training and two missions. I love it when people come up to me and say, "I am so happy to meet a real, live astronaut." I smile and think, "I'm the one who is happy—happy to be alive."

When facing long odds, fear of failure is a natural response. Yet as Franklin D. Roosevelt said when faced with the daunting task of pulling America out of the Great Depression, "The only thing we have to fear is fear itself."

Remember, it is not failure that defines us, but our ability to rise above it. We must focus on what's happening now rather than dwell on past failures or disappointments. Accept what is, and move on in a positive way. As Gene Kranz, the flight controller of *Apollo 13*, was famously quoted as saying in the movie about that rescue, "Failure is not an option." Your best option is to transform your failures into victory by learning from past mistakes and moving forward to realize your full potential. As author and businessman Mark Fisher points out, "When you overcome your fears, your power becomes unlimited. You tap into the multi-potential being that you are."

—

I discovered early in life that I am a lifelong learner. I simply like learning new things. I believe that when you think you know it all, you are dead. Or at least you might as well be, because you are setting yourself up for failure. Not surprisingly, education was the enabler of my achievement and success. But when I joined the astronaut program, I was placed in a new learning environment—an environment where failure is not an option.

The *Apollo 13* incident required the team members to step forward, take the lead, and make individual contributions. As a result, their success became symbolic of the team's refusal to accept failure. These ideas have become part of the culture at NASA.

Even though I had gone through college and medical training, this was a new arena—to fly in space, an entirely different skill set was required. So, I had to step up to the plate and do things that I had never done before, such as survival training. At NASA I learned to become part of a team. I overcame the uncertainty about my ability to survive the rigor of training. I became part of a "we" and got total immersed in the culture.

One technique I used to overcome the uneasiness I felt in doing something different, in stepping into the unknown, was to fill that void with knowledge. When you attempt something new, it challenges you and forces you to grow.

—

Change in life is certain, and leaving NASA when I did challenged me. Over the years, I have talked to many people who are afraid of change. This fear is simply the fear of the unknown. What's around the corner or around the bend? This is always a scary question, even for me. Sometimes we must simply open the hatch and step out on faith.

Of all the things that I have done in my life up to this point, becoming an entrepreneur was by far the most stressful. Yes, it's true: Being launched on a rocket was less challenging than dealing with the intricacies of private business. Initially, the most difficult part was dealing with my fellow vice presidents and battling for position within the company. I learned that Sun Tzu's great sixth-century military treatise, *The Art of War,* applies equally to the battlefield and the board room. After four years of constant internal battles and attempts at trying to rise in the ranks, I lost. Not knowing how the game was played, and tired of competing with men and women who had been in the game much longer, I finally sought a different path to entrepreneurship. I was fortunate to have met Jack Gill, Bob Ulrich, and others during my transition into the venture capital world. With their help, I was able to rise above my limitations. I was able to build upon my past successes and failures in order to try something different. A few years later I found JoAnn Price, a very successful business-woman who not only had built a multibillion-dollar firm, but also was willing to assist venture capitalists like me. I owe these individuals and others for my career in business, and I thank them sincerely.

However, although generous people may give you advice and encouragement, they cannot do the work for you—the work that it takes to build a successful firm. That, you must do for yourself. Was it easy? No way. Was it exciting? You bet! I learned a great deal in the process. In this business there are many opportunities. The first trick is to know when to invest and with whom. The second trick is to avoid compromising your integrity and principles.

Shortly after starting the company, one of the leading venture capital magazines interviewed me, wanting to know why I had traded in my astronaut suit for a business suit. That was a very good question. After thinking about it for a few seconds, I came to the conclusion that these two "suits" actually had a number of similarities. Both professions required the ability to manage risks, both were challenging to the human spirit, and both provided the opportunity for tremendous rewards.

Why do I like venture capital? First, I like discovering new things, particularly advanced technology that can positively impact people and the world.

Second, I recognize that I am at my best when opening doors and bringing people together to generate new ideas and create new ways to do things. I surround myself with people who are like-minded—those who want the same things that I want, but who have different but complementary skills. In this way, I am able to utilize each individual's talents to create a team whose total abilities exceed those of any single player.

Finally, a large part of my role as a venture capitalist is to work to amass wealth. But it is not all about the money . . . it's about what you do with it. You can use wealth to improve people's lives, improve communities, and improve our society.

I am now able to contribute to the community through the application of new technology, invest in people and their dreams, and at the same time build wealth. My own goal is to be a venture capitalist of life. I want to become rich in all things: knowledge, wealth, health, family, love, and God.

—

Family is very important to me. Family stays with you all your life. No matter what type of family you come from, once you realize their importance you will be able to use that awareness for good. Family can help you overcome the negative forces in your life.

One aspect of family that has always haunted me is the fact that my biological father was not a part of my life. As a child I spent a great deal of time wondering why. I never felt, as many kids do, that I had something to do with the breakup of my parents' marriage. I knew what the issues were, and I respected my mother for her strength. But I wondered what it would be like to have my father as a part of my life.

At age eighteen, I went looking for my father. I found him in Philadelphia, still caught up in the same things that had caused problems in his marriage. Despite this, he was an extremely nice man, and I could see why my mother fell in love with him. We stayed in contact off and on over the years. When I was in my late twenties, he had a spiritual experience; he discovered God, and his drinking days were over. It certainly improved our relationship, but there was still a distance between us, and in some ways it is still there today.

As I reflect back on this, I realize how important he has been in my life despite not always being there. After all, he is my biological father. Many of his ways and mannerisms are similar to mine—others comment on it when we are together. The failures that I see in him as a father, I have transmuted into my professional achievements. For there is a part of me that says, "I am never going to be like my father." But in many ways, many good ways, I am exactly like him. My sister always says, "You can't change where you have come from," to which I add, "You can't change your genetics." The only thing you can do is learn to live with the world you have been given and change it where you can. That's exactly what I have tried to do over the years.

But sometimes learning to live with change can be difficult. I fell in love with a bright, beautiful woman who became my wife for nineteen years. Even now, I cannot say what drew me to her or brought us together. But circumstances led to the end of our union in 2008. To this day I still love her deeply. Love is the counterpoint to the disorder of life. It makes us stronger by helping us discover who we really are.

Sandra and I have a daughter, Alexandria, now seventeen and headed soon for college, who will forever bond us. Alex has her mother's beauty and, I hope, her intellect.

There are losses along life's winding road. But this one is personal, not part of the public story I have told countless times, in countless venues. Nevertheless, I remain blessed to have had the experience of marriage. The older I get and the more time I have for reflection, the more I come to know that things happen for a reason.

—

I believe that fulfilling your dreams is the ultimate high. To be able to honestly say that I set a goal and accomplished it is a high greater than any you can imagine. I have had several highs in life, as a physician, an astronaut, and a venture capitalist. And I thank God every day for these blessings!

When was the last time you attended a musical concert where a band or an orchestra was playing and you truly listened? If you really paid attention, you probably noticed that the band was made up of individual members who are each talented on their individual instruments. Alone, their individual parts may not make sense, but together they make beautiful music that touches the hearts of those listening. In this state we are all caught up in the moment and the music, feeling that we are a part of the universe that encompasses all that is good in life. We are on top of the world; nothing is wrong and everything is in order. What a great feeling . . . a tremendous view . . . endless joy!

This is a state we all seek, a state of mind that says we can conquer all and overcome anything. If we focus on becoming the best that we can be, knowing who we are, and understanding our role in life and in the universe, then we find not only our own individual truth but also the truth that contributes to all of society. If we play our own instrument the very best we can, then we become part of a symphony much greater than ourselves, and we live our lives in harmony with the universe. This is why it is so important to reach your full potential! This is how important you are to the world. There is a passage in the Bible that says it the best:

> The Spirit Himself bears witness with our spirit that we are children of God, and if children, heirs also of God and fellow-heirs with Christ . . . For the anxious longing of the creation waits eagerly for the revealing of the sons of God.
> —Romans 8:16–19

I have shared my experiences in an attempt to encourage others whose lives have been less fortunate. No question, good fortune has played an important role in mine. Being in the right place at the right time, meeting the right people, taking advantage of opportunities as they present themselves—all this has been part of it.

I had dinner recently with some people whom I would classify as bona fide intellectuals and academics. They were university professors and businessmen and -women. We talked about a number of things, but ended up in a discussion about the origins of life. We had the usual dialogue about creation versus evolution. But we ended on a very interesting note: I asked the self-appointed leader of this conversation who had started it all, "Do you believe in God?" He is a man whom I respect, but I thought he would not admit his beliefs in public. He simply said, "Yes!"

In his opinion and mine, God exists in everything that we see, hear, touch, and feel. God is omnipresent! Think about it: the only thing that great scientists really do is describe the world that already exists. We do not create anything that has not already existed.

Traveling in space gave me a profound new perspective as I gazed down on our planet. From that height, you get the so-called God's-eye view, which allows you to see the world as never before and affirms what I have believed for so long.

When I returned to the relative comforts of the space shuttle *Discovery* on that day in February 1995, there was a phone call waiting for me from the president of the United States, Bill Clinton. He had called to congratulate me on my walk in space. I told him, brimming with adrenaline and self-confidence, "I may be the first, Mr. President, but I won't be the last." In fact I wasn't. Since my historic walk, a number of African-Americans have not only walked in space but also set records for the next generation. I am proud to have represented the country in such a way.

I would like everyone I meet to experience the feeling of accomplishment as I have. To have a dream and see it fulfilled through hard work and determination, despite social and economic status. To try, and if you fail, to learn from the lessons this world has to offer.

—

Years after I started Vesalius Ventures, I was asked by a local university to provide internships to its MBA students. One of the interns I selected was a very smart young man who, I soon learned, lacked direction. His journey had been driven by the expectations of others—his parents, his friends, and anyone else he thought was important. As a result, he went from one thing to the next, without a plan. It would be fun for a while, and then he would look for the next interesting thing. I finally pulled him into my office and asked him a question: "Do you know what you want to do when you grow up?" He had no idea. He just liked having fun and hanging out with his friends. That is an okay attitude when you are an undergraduate student, but when you are approaching thirty, it can be a problem. He never felt the need to settle down and make a real decision. He soon found himself in a predicament—one, I believe, that was rooted in his fear of failure and his lack of direction.

The plain truth is, we really do live in a nation of limitless possibilities and opportunities. We just need to leave our fears behind and go after them. And that, I believe, is what life is all about.

I worry about the future of America because I cannot imagine what would happen if the richest, strongest, freest country in the world lost its drive and competitiveness. Yet as our nation struggles to recover from its worst economic crisis since the Great

Depression, we are at grave risk of losing our technical edge to increasingly capable global competitors. If we do not take more "giant steps," this is indeed what will happen.

The prosperity we are striving to revive is a product of past commitments to education and our investments in science and technology. The decline in our international standing begins with our hesitation to renew these efforts. We must expect more from our policymakers, educators, and children when it comes to proficiency in science, technology, engineering, and mathematics, the STEM fields that keep us atop the economic pinnacle.

I have argued this case in these pages and elsewhere, on podiums, in interviews, and in what the press calls "op-ed pieces." I repeat them now because my concerns remain the same, as does my optimism that we can and will rise above our fears and our challenges.

I flew on the space shuttle twice, and my extraterrestrial mission was to serve as a mission specialist, crew medical officer, and payload commander and to walk in space. I accomplished my dream. My terrestrial mission as a civilian is to ensure that young Americans have the same opportunity to follow their dreams. This was the message I carried into the inner cities and rural areas, into public and private institutions, into homes and conventions. From this vantage point, I view the country from the ground up.

In a country where one student drops out of school every twenty-six seconds, totaling seven thousand students per day, and more than 1.2 million per year, action must be taken to reverse the effects of this tragedy. Our country needs citizens who will be prepared to compete across the globe. It is an issue that affects every one of us.

Through my foundation and our programs, we have provided students a preview of the college experience and the skills for success, and we have empowered their dreams. America needs to wake up to the realization that we are no longer the only leaders in the world. We are outmanned by a number of countries, such as China and India, in the number of scientists and engineers that we produce. In 2005, Gereffi and Wadhwa researched the annual production of engineers, computer scientists, and information technology specialists at the bachelor's degree and sub-baccalaureate levels to create an accurate and representative comparison of the numbers of engineers produced annually in each of the three countries. They found that the United States graduated seventy thousand engineers a year, compared to three hundred and fifty thousand from India and six hundred thousand from China.

We were once a country of inventors. In 2008, according to the U.S. Patent and Trademark Office, 50 percent of the patents issued in the United States were owned by foreign governments, compared to 37 percent twenty years earlier. We have lost the motivation for discovery. Many of our children have become complacent and idle, unable and unwilling to do what it takes to achieve. The question is, why? I do not have all the answers, but I am convinced that the desire for instant gratification is a significant part of the problem.

We must instill in our young people the value of hard work in achieving their dreams. The question that should be asked now is, how do we change the mind-set of our youth from acting like radios, sending and never receiving? How do we change them from being consumed by video games to becoming leaders in technology, from being passive to becoming active in their own growth?

Despite the negatives, as I travel the country meeting a new generation of kids, I am encouraged by what I see. When I look into their eyes, I see many with a desire to learn, who simply need guidance and nurturing. If we do not make this investment now, we lose the future. Each time a dream goes unfulfilled, and we lose the brainpower of one, we lose the collective contribution for all.

America has long prided itself as a nation of dreamers, a land where everyone can strive for a better life, a place where grand achievements such as top-notch universities, missions to the moon, personal computers, and the Internet spring forth to create a new prosperity. Space exploration, among the most difficult of human endeavors, can only serve to enlarge our economic sphere so that it is rich with the promise of new technologies for other pursuits.

For years my friends and advisers have encouraged me to write my autobiography. But some might say that "The Life and Times of Bernard A. Harris Jr." would only serve to enlarge an already overinflated ego. Point taken. So I wanted this book to be something a little different. Yes, I have recounted my experiences and accomplishments, but I included a generous dose of my thoughts, feelings, opinions, doubts, and, yes, my fears. My hope is that as you read this book, you will use these experiences that transformed my life as a useful model for yours.

Most important, I hope to help those who are feeling lost, those trying to find themselves, and those who want to make a difference. I hope that this book conveys the story of a man on a mission: to become all that I can be in my limited time on this Earth. It is a mission of self-discovery that has carried me from modest beginnings to soar higher than I could have ever dreamed. My lasting wish is that my narrative will motivate, inspire, enlighten, and empower you, too.

Appendix

THE HARRIS FOUNDATION

Founded in 1998, The Harris Foundation (THF) is a 501(c)(3), nonprofit organization based in Houston, Texas. The foundation's overall mission is to invest in community-based initiatives to support education, health, and wealth. THF supports programs that empower individuals—in particular minorities and those who are economically or socially disadvantaged—to recognize their potential and pursue their dreams.

The Harris Foundation uses its own unique brand to address the major national issues of education, health, and wealth. Striving to empower minorities, the underrepresented, and other disadvantaged populations, the foundation programs reach beyond students to encompass parents, teachers, and communities—all working together to make a difference. Through our interactive STEM education, health programs, and wealth programs, we expose students and communities to new ideas and prepare them for the future.

Vision of Success

The vision of The Harris Foundation is to prepare a pipeline of young people and communities that are prepared to meet the future requirements of our nation. By utilizing positive role models to increase student impact and life success in our hands-on work with communities, The Harris Foundation promotes six principles:

- Encouraging education in science, technology, engineering, and mathematics
- Building financial skills
- Motivating youth to stay in school
- Fostering youth leadership and citizenship
- Instilling the values of responsibility, fairness, and respect
- Promoting optimum health

We work hand-in-hand with communities and use positive role models to increase student impact and life success.

The Education Mission

The Harris Foundation education programs enable youth to develop and achieve their full potential through the support of social, recreational, and educational programs for grades kindergarten through 12. Through three primary initiatives—the DREAM Tour, the ExxonMobil Bernard Harris Summer Science Camp, and Dare to Dream—the foundation encourages math and science education, motivates youth to stay in school, fosters youth leadership and citizenship, and instills the values of responsibility, fairness, and respect. Recently, The Harris Foundation and ExxonMobil have created a new award program with the Council of the Great City Schools, called the ExxonMobil Bernard Harris Math and Science Scholarship Program. It awards college scholarships to graduating seniors.

We believe that students can be prepared now for the careers of the future through a structured education program and the use of positive role models. Over the past ten years, the foundation has worked closely with NASA, ExxonMobil, and others to inspire and motivate students to pursue careers in science, technology, engineering, and mathematics and to ensure a pipeline of people who are prepared to meet the requirements for the nation. More than twenty thousand K-through-12 students participate in and benefit from THF programs annually.

Dare to Dream

Established in 1995, Dare to Dream (DTD) is a nine-month, elementary-school-based program that boosts self-esteem in children by providing them access to positive role models. Co-sponsored by the Harris County Juvenile Probation Department, Communities in Schools, and local area school districts, the program uses interactive math and science curriculum, as well as career discussions with astronauts and other professionals, to get students thinking about their future and exploring the exciting possibilities.

The program kicks off each year with a visit from Dr. Bernard Harris, who distributes cards with his personal credo—the ABCs, which stands for "I can Achieve, if I Believe and Conceive my dream." During the first semester, a biweekly curriculum is designed to teach students about respect, responsibility, and other values. The second-semester curriculum focuses on introducing students to interesting and exciting career fields. Juvenile probation officers volunteer to visit the schools regularly, reinforcing Harris's message of the ABCs as well as the need for self-esteem, responsibility, and getting along with others. During the entire year, students also perform at least two community service projects. They maintain journals that are monitored by school officials for progress. In the end, DTD results in students having an increased desire to stay in school, dreaming of successful careers, and setting their goals for achievement.

The DREAM Tour

The DREAM (Daring to Reach Excellence for America's Minds) Tour is exactly what THF is promoting throughout the country to the youth of America. Through the support of the ExxonMobil Foundation, the goal is to reach one million students, parents, and teachers in order to highlight the need for mathematics and science education. This outreach program is held year-round to provide a platform for a national dialogue; to inspire and motivate students to pursue careers in science, technology, engineering, and mathematics; and to ensure a pipeline of people who are prepared to meet the economic requirements of the nation.

The DREAM Tour program is an action-packed one-hour segment that includes a motivational message delivered by Dr. Bernard Harris. Upon conclusion of the program, Dr. Harris meets with thirty of the local top math and science students for a thirty-minute question and answer opportunity. Starting in January 2009, the tour added a component called the Education Forum: Listening to America. The Education Forum is an opportunity to meet with local educators, business associates in the STEM fields, parents, teachers, superintendents, and others. The purpose of the forum is to create a dialogue with the guests in order to share their opinions and thoughts on STEM and where they feel the students are academically in these related fields. While these forums on STEM education discuss barriers and obstacles, they do so with the intention of becoming a catalyst for change, identifying key strategies and partnerships that will allow this call to action to lead to real change. Some of the key highlights can be found on The Harris Foundation website.

The ExxonMobil Bernard Harris Summer Science Camp

Established in 1993, the Bernard Harris Summer Science Camp/Saturday Academy is an annual two-week residential camp that gives middle school students the opportunity to enhance their proficiency in math and science. The camps are a collaborative partnership of The Harris Foundation and the ExxonMobil Foundation, in conjunction with universities and school districts. The ExxonMobil Bernard Harris Summer Science Camp, a free academic program of The Harris Foundation, takes an active role in shaping science, technology, engineering, and mathematics (STEM) education in students entering grade six, seven, or eight. The mission is to enable all youth, particularly historically underserved and underrepresented students with limited opportunities, to develop and achieve their full potential and dreams.

The program is hosted on thirty university campuses across the nation. The following descriptions of some of the camps show student reactions and highlights.

Lamar University, Beaumont, Texas: "We built the *Titanic!*" giggled the children in a group that named itself the Dominant Brains. They were told to complete a model of a raft within fifteen minutes that would hold the largest number of pennies without sinking in a tub of water. Kyle Leyendecker, a camp counselor and Lamar graduate, helped the sixth-, seventh- and eighth-graders build the rafts out of two sheets of aluminum foil and plastic straws. "We don't think it's gonna hold a lot of pennies," said eleven-year-old Tracey Carter. "The aluminum is real thin." But the larger purpose was served. "We got to teach the children about science and how it can be used in everyday instances," said the camp director, Otilia Urbina.

Northeastern University, Boston, Massachusetts: Science, technology, engineering, and math probably aren't the first subjects that come to middle schoolers' minds when they think of summer vacation. But for forty-eight Boston-area students, taking part in a science camp at Northeastern University might just be the key to a brighter future. Beyond the figures and formulas, however, there was traditional summer fun to be had. Splitting into sixteen teams, students watched the makeshift bottle rockets they had constructed launch into the afternoon sky. The winning team's rocket remained airborne for 6.1 seconds.

Oregon State, Corvallis: The campers hosted a special guest: Dr. Bernard Harris Jr. himself. He was the first black astronaut to walk in space, but the students found him to be down-to-earth. He mingled and chatted with them as they performed science experiments and ate lunch. He also signed autographs. "It was amazing," said Adam Case of Medford, who will start eighth grade in the fall. "I've never seen an actual astronaut." Adam was eager to learn about engineering because he hopes to be a builder someday. The teams actually built structures to scale out of wood and duct tape.

Many of the adolescents were thrilled to be staying in the dorms. "It makes you feel like you're a college kid, kind of," said Daniel Garcia-Archundia, who wants to be a doctor, maybe a pediatrician. Daniel said his favorite thing about the camp was the food. "But all the teachers are really cool," he added.

University of Southern California, Los Angeles: Dozens of eyes opened a little wider as the imposing figure opened the floor to questions. Most of the fifty middle school students from the neighborhoods around USC wanted to know all about eating, sleeping, and going to the bathroom in space, questions that astronaut Bernard Harris has fielded many times before.

Then one of the children asked if Dr. Harris, the first African-American to walk in space and a veteran of two shuttle missions, had any other goals to accomplish. While this is not a question he hears often, it was one he was ready to answer. "The only reason I am here," he said, "is because of a dream I had when I was your age. Dreams are powerful. There is no greater high than having a goal, a dream, fulfilled." His ultimate goal is to have students believing that they actually can be doctors, scientists, engineers, even astronauts. "My goal is to see 100 percent of them graduate from high school and 100 percent of them go on to college. Expectations are set too low. We have to raise the bar."

University of Virginia, Charlottesville: The students' excitement grew as each group brought its boat forward to be put in a vat of water and loaded, one by one, with pennies. The winning boat, a wide, flat model designed by the Ducks team, held 192 pennies before taking on water. David Evans, an associate professor of computer science at UVA, gave the students a lesson on cryptography, using a black pirate chest, a gift bag, and a couple of padlocks. It took several passes before the kids learned they could only get at the box, representing information, by having the key to the padlock, which represented encryption. Jared Capelle, a rising sixth-grader, said, "It's amazing. It was a lot of work, but it wasn't hard." He sent in his application in December and was accepted in June. "It just sounded like fun," said Jared, who is interested in plants, animals, and robotics.

New Jersey Institute of Technology, Newark: "It's okay to be a geek, because geeks rule the world," astronaut Bernard Harris told fifty-two middle school students at the summer science camp that bears his name and is funded by ExxonMobil. Dr. Harris, a physician-turned-astronaut, challenged the youngsters, as they noshed on fried-chicken-and-brownie lunches, to consider careers in science, technology, engineering, and/or math, a grouping often referred to as STEM. "Each of you was born into this world with infinite possibilities," said Harris. "Only you can decide what your special talent is." He related his own story, including how he applied to NASA to become an astronaut and was one out of six thousand applicants. Only 150 were offered interviews, and only twenty-three were offered jobs.

The students hailed from thirty-six school districts around the state and typically represented the academic crème de la crème, since admission to the camp is based on merit. Make the cut, though, and the two-week summer residency is free. "I really liked being here," explained thirteen-year-old Chase Upshaw, who will start eighth grade in Liberty Middle School, in West Orange. "I learned in robotics how to program a robot. Now my robot can complete tasks like moving rocks from one area to another." A lesson in math about gears and how they work also captivated him. Paras Shah, of East Brunswick, gave points to the Liberty Science Center trips as well as an excursion to ExxonMobil. "My favorite," he said, "was when the engineers taught us how to make silly putty by combining glue, water, and Borax."

Temple University, Philadelphia, Pennsylvania: Science camper Hannah Rifkin, thirteen, is an eighth-grader at Sandy Run Middle School. Hannah said she has enjoyed the camp because she got to work on hands-on projects such as catapults and solar-paneled toy cars. "It has been fun, and I love science," she said. Camp volunteer Barb Carfolite said she enjoyed teaching the students about the Archimedes principle of buoyancy and preparing them for the raft competition. Others designed modules for two missions to Mars, one with people aboard and one without. Barb added "I hope that they take with them the fact that science is alive and not just an observation."

University of Oklahoma, Norman: Former astronaut Bernard Harris explained that in space, even orange juice can have zero gravity and float in the shape of a ball. "It spins, just like the Earth, and it gains speed," said Dr. Harris. He said he blew a hole through it, making a brief doughnut shape before the juice went back into a ball. The commanding officer then yelled at him; Harris put his lips to the juice ball and drank it. The mesmerized middle school students smiled as he described the event.

This was the first year the camp had been held at OU, and the students were separated into three groups. Each of the groups spent about one hour focusing on a specific area of study, including lab exercises, research, and field studies at the Wichita Mountains and Lake Texoma. "The thing we like about the program," said Harris, "is that science is spoken here. It's okay to be smart." Jesse Herrera, an eleven-year-old, agreed. "It's really fun," said Jesse. "We get to go swimming today!"

The Health Mission

The Harris Foundation's health education programs focus on improving overall health, promoting wellness, and increasing prevention in communities throughout the nation. The first program in health was formed through THF's relationship with the Robert Wood Johnson Foundation (RWJF).

The RWJF Community Health Leaders (CHL) goal is to

provide recognition for the contributions that community health leaders make to achieving RWJF's mission and goals and to enhance their capacity to have a more permanent and widespread impact on health problems.

The CHL program each year honors ten outstanding and otherwise unrecognized individuals who overcome daunting odds to expand access to health care and social services to underserved populations in communities across the United States. The program aims to elevate the work of these unsung heroes through enhanced recognition, technical assistance, and leadership development opportunities.

The program has the following goals:

- Increased national exposure for leaders, through media and partnerships with other national organizations
  - Annual selection of ten community health leaders, including a one-time financial award of $125,000 to each leader. The award comprises $105,000 to support the leader's initiative and $20,000 as a personal gift to the leader in recognition of his or her contributions
  - Promote CHL participation on national and federal advisory committees, grant review teams, etc.
  - Partnerships with select national organizations to place CHL on meeting agendas for presentations, establish Internet linkages, and encourage nominations
  - Create panels of leaders to review and analyze the

role and impact of community health leadership on select current health and social policies in communities and neighborhoods

- Increase CHL capacity and relationships in order to utilize skills and tools (e.g., measurement, scale)
  - Technical assistance through consultation, phone and video-conferencing, and connections to other resources and expertise
  - Participation in an annual meeting for all leaders, and periodic regional meetings or conventions
  - Participation in leader-facilitated work groups that focus on current issues
  - Peer exchanges among leaders to share relevant expertise
  - Sponsored participation and scholarships at conferences and meetings of specific interest and value
- Facilitate communication with other RWJF programs and staff resources
  - Focus groups on RWJF interest areas
  - Collaborations and referrals between RWJF programs and grantees
  - CHL presentations at program staff meetings
  - Consultations with RWJF teams, as appropriate

The Wealth Mission

The Harris Foundation plans to launch wealth education programs that teach students, primarily in high school, about sound financial principles, beginning with entrepreneurship.

For more information:

The Harris Foundation
info@theharrisfoundation.org
www.theharrisfoundation.org

ACKNOWLEDGMENTS

I have many people to thank for the writing of this book. At the top of the list is my mother. Through her courage, I was able to escape the environment that may have resulted in an entirely different outcome for my life. I am indebted to her, and eventually to my stepfather as well, for providing my siblings and me with a nurturing upbringing. Their guidance and support allowed the three of us to be successful. When people ask her about her children, my mother swells with pride to say, "All of them are doing well. I have a son who is executive director of a large government organization; a daughter who is a nurse who taught nursing and started her own business; and, of course, my son the astronaut." Indeed, she is proud, and so she should be, given where we started in life. I am proud to have her as my mother.

I owe my self-confidence to my mother; my internal compass to my sister, who has been my spiritual guide through the years; and my courage to my brother and stepfather. My sincere thanks to my friends, old and new, and my family, especially my daughter, Alex, whose love and support have given me strength.

I have had a blessed life. I have traveled and interacted with people all over the world. I have told my story countless times and in many different venues in an attempt to encourage those who would listen to my story. For years I have been encouraged by others to write an autobiography. Instead of doing a book filled with self-gratifying accounts of my life, I have chosen to write a book that, in essence, captures my life but reflects the many transitions of my existence on this Earth. Life has a way of giving us unexpected twists and turns as a result of the challenges of simply living in this world. This book is a collection of my experiences, my thoughts, my feelings, and my opinions. It is these things that have made me the person I am today . . . a physician, an astronaut, and an entrepreneur.

When I finally decided that I would tackle this book project, I needed to find a place where I could pull it all together. That place was the Triple Creek Ranch in Montana. This ranch is one of the most picturesque places in the world. From Texas, it is a full day's travel: first a flight to Missoula, and then a seventy-mile car ride south to the base of the Bitterroot Mountains. The peace and solitude I found there allowed me to focus on completing the outline, the proposal, and the draft for this book. I was inspired by the beautiful scenery of the mountains and running streams. I thoroughly enjoyed the hiking, running, and horseback riding. My only challenge was recovering from a day in the saddle, herding cattle on the working ranch. We moved about five hundred head, and in the ensuing days, I found it difficult to get up and down from a chair. This relegated me to sitting most of the time, so I had no excuse but to complete the task at hand. I would like to thank my dear friends Barbara and Craig Barrett for allowing me to stay at their home at Triple Creek Ranch.

My gratitude also goes to Jim and Marsha Lamb, who

encouraged me to pursue this goal—so much so that Jim lent me his expertise as a writer. He gave me guidance on many aspects of the book and provided the editing of my initial concept.

My passion these days centers on where the United States of America is headed. In particular, I am concerned about how we will remain valuable contributors to this world—how we will continue to be the leaders of technology and innovation. My conclusion is that it requires a significant investment in our youth and their communities. Many people share this passion, for example, Gerald McElvy and Truman Bell. Since our early days together at the University of Houston, Gerald and I have always had the common goal of creating opportunities for America's youth. As president of the ExxonMobil Foundation, he was responsible for introducing me to Truman and ExxonMobil. I am indeed grateful for their partnership, which has resulted in the education programs we now offer throughout the nation.

In addition, I would like to thank Andy Stern for his marketing guidance and for introducing me to Mickey Herskowitz. Mickey is a prolific writer who has been involved with the autobiographies of such famous people as Dan Rather, Mickey Mantle, Howard Cosell, Bette Davis, Shirley Jones and Marty Ingels, Gene Tierney, Gene Autry, Nolan Ryan, Tom Kite, and John Connally—to name a few. I am indeed honored to have his talents applied to my autobiography.

An estimated 600 million people in forty-three countries watched Neil Armstrong take his "small step" onto the surface of the moon. The date was July 20, 1969, and for me the image was frozen in time—at 8:55 p.m.—in New Mexico, where I lay spellbound on the living room floor, my chin cupped in my hands.

Armstrong's words have been quoted so often, there is no need to repeat them here. But for me, what became a footnote to the lunar landing echoes just as clearly.

The *Apollo 8* mission, commanded by Frank Borman, had orbited the moon during Christmas week in 1968, giving humans a chance for the first time to see the planet Earth photographed as a complete entity from outer space. But the lingering memory is that of the crew doing a shared reading of the first chapter of Genesis on Christmas Eve—a perfectly timed surprise, as the lunar module pilot, William Anders, began softly:

In the beginning God created the heavens and the Earth, and the Earth was without form, and void, and darkness was upon the face of the deep . . . And God said, "Let there be light," and there was light.

God has played a significant role in my life. So, when the opportunity avails itself to get a different perspective, a higher perspective from which to look at life, I feel that one must take it. I was blessed to have had the opportunity to view the world plain and clear, without inhibitions or limitations . . . a world of possibilities and opportunities. I thank God for the opportunities and the many blessings I have received.

My motive for writing this book is to motivate and inspire all people. My intention is to enlighten and empower—to encouraging individuals to fulfill their own destiny, just as my mission has been to become all that I could be in the limited time I have on this Earth. My mission of self-discovery has carried me from modest beginnings to soar to unbelievable heights. So, as I recount my adventure and the path, it provides an opportunity for you, the reader, to examine your own life. My life is an example of what can be accomplished with the right attitude, because with the right attitude, your altitude has no limit.

ABOUT THE AUTHORS

Bernard A. Harris Jr. was born in Temple, Texas, and raised on the Navajo Nation during his formative years. After his family moved back to Texas, he graduated from Sam Houston High School in San Antonio in 1974.

He holds a bachelor of science in biology from the University of Houston, a master of medical science from the University of Texas Medical Branch at Galveston, a master of business administration from the University of Houston Clear Lake, and a doctorate of medicine from the Texas Tech University School of Medicine.

Dr. Harris completed a residency in internal medicine at the Mayo Clinic and a National Research Council Fellowship in endocrinology at the NASA Ames Research Center, and he trained as a flight surgeon at the Aerospace School of Medicine, Brooks Air Force Base, in San Antonio. He is also a licensed private pilot and certified scuba diver.

The several faculty appointments Dr. Harris has held include associate professor in internal medicine at the University of Texas Medical Branch and assistant professor at Baylor College of Medicine. Additionally, he is the author and coauthor of numerous scientific publications.

Dr. Harris was at NASA for ten years in such positions as

clinical scientist, flight surgeon, and astronaut. He conducted research in musculoskeletal physiology and disuse osteoporosis, and as a result, he helped develop countermeasures and in-flight medical devices for space adaptation and the extension of astronaut stays in space. Selected into the Astronaut Corps in January 1990, Dr. Harris was a mission specialist on the space shuttle *Columbia* STS-55/Spacelab D-2 in 1993. As payload commander on space shuttle *Discovery* STS-63 in 1995, he served on the first flight of the joint Russian-American Space Program, becoming the first African-American to walk in space. In his time as an astronaut, he he has logged more than 438 hours and traveled more than 7.2 million miles in space.

His various roles in private industry range from vice president and chief scientist to vice president of business development to president and CEO. Dr. Harris has served on boards and committees at state, federal, and private institutions.

Currently, Dr. Harris is CEO and managing partner of Vesalius Ventures, a venture capital firm investing in the future of health care. He is also the founder of The Harris Foundation, a nonprofit organization that supports math/science education and health and wealth programs for youth and their communities.

Throughout his career, Dr. Harris has received numerous awards and recognitions, including four honorary doctorate degrees, two NASA Space Flight medals, the 2000 Horatio Alger Award, and election as Fellow of the American College of Physicians.

Mickey Herskowitz is a Houston-based author and nationally known sports columnist. He currently holds an endowed journalism chair at Sam Houston State University. He has written or helped write fifty-one books, including seven bestsellers.

Like Dr. Harris, Mr. Herskowitz is a distinguished alumnus of the University of Houston.